P9-DGT-129

CLINICAL EVALUATIONS OF SCHOOL-AGED CHILDREN

A Structured Approach to the Diagnosis of Child and Adolescent Mental Disorders

Second Edition

SUSAN K. SAMUELS / SUSANA SIKORSKY

Professional Resource Press
Sarasota, Florida

Published by Professional Resource Press
(An imprint of Professional Resource Exchange, Inc.)
Post Office Box 15560
Sarasota, FL 34277-1560

The copy editor for this book was David Anson, the typesetter was Denise Franck, the managing editor was Debra Fink, and the cover designer was Laurie Girsch.

Library of Congress Cataloging-in-Publication Data

Samuels, Susan K.
    Clinical evaluations of school-aged children : a structured
approach to the diagnosis of child and adolescent mental disorders /
Susan K. Samuels, Susana Sikorsky. -- 2nd ed.
        p.   cm.
    Includes bibliographical references and index.
    ISBN 1-56887-027-2 (alk. paper)
    1. Mental illness--Diagnosis. 2. Child psychopathology.
3. Adolescent psychopathology. I. Sikorsky, Susana. II. Title.
    [DNLM: 1. Mental Disorders--diagnosis case studies. 2. Mental
Disorders--in infancy & childhood case studies. 3. Mental
Disorders--in adolescence case studies.   WS 350 S1935c 1998]
RJ503.5.S25 1998
618.92'89075--dc21
DNLM/DLC
for Library of Congress   98-11269
                                                                    CIP

ACKNOWLEDGMENT

Our gratitude to our professional colleagues in our local school districts and around the state of Connecticut for sharing their expertise, and graciously supporting this endeavor.

94697

TABLE OF CONTENTS

MOOD DISORDERS *(Cont'd)*

ADJUSTMENT DISORDERS

PERVASIVE DEVELOPMENTAL DISORDERS

FEEDING AND EATING DISORDERS

ELIMINATION DISORDERS

SLEEP DISORDERS

TIC DISORDERS

INTRODUCTION

The *Clinical Evaluations of School-Aged Children: A Structured Approach to the Diagnosis of Child and Adolescent Mental Disorders,* first published in 1990, has been revised in order to update diagnoses according to the *Diagnostic and Statistical Manual of Mental Disorders - Fourth Edition (DSM-IV),* published in 1994 by the American Psychiatric Association. The main purpose of this book remains unchanged. Mental health professionals in schools need to communicate with a number of other professionals, such as psychiatrists and clinical psychologists involved in the assessment, diagnosis, and treatment of mental disorders in children and adolescents. Theoretical background, knowledge, experience, and practices among such professionals vary considerably, resulting in an array of differing terminology to describe a child's behavior and emotional status. The second edition of *Clinical Evaluations of School-Aged Children* was created to bring about some uniformity in the behavioral considerations necessary for a given diagnosis.

Mental health professionals in schools must gather data, refine evaluations, respond to referral sources, prepare reports for clinical consultations, and interpret clinical findings to parents and school staff. One of the problems in communication between school personnel and outside professionals is the wide variation of terms used in the two different settings. Because most reports from clinicians include terms from the *DSM-IV,* knowledge of the specific criteria associated with each syndrome is necessary for school professionals as consultants in the school setting and liaison between schools and clinical practitioners.

Clinical Evaluations of School-Aged Children (2nd ed.) focuses on the child and adolescent syndromes described in the *DSM-IV.* Certain syndromes such as Learning Disorders (which include Reading Disorder, Mathematics Disorder, and Disorder of Written Expression) as well as Motor Skills Disorder and Expressive Language Disorder were excluded from this book. The criteria for determining abnormality in the above-mentioned areas vary considerably among states and school districts according to their particular diagnostic guidelines and policies. The diagnostic category of Mental Retardation has also been excluded from this book. In general, such diagnoses of primarily intellectual/academic deficiencies are routinely addressed by school personnel and do not necessarily warrant outside clinical consultation. Also excluded from the *Clinical Evaluations of School-Aged Children (2nd ed.)* are all Substance-Related Disorders. The practitioner should, however, investigate the use of substances by the referred child since their effects may mask or mimic mental or behavioral conditions.

As the intent of this book is to clarify, differentiate, and cluster behaviors into well-defined syndromes, we have also excluded Unspecified or Not Otherwise Specified diagnoses. Such classifications can be used by clinical practitioners when there are insufficient data or the data available do not meet the full criteria for a given diagnosis (*DSM-IV*). In addition to the inclusion of all syndromes under the general category of Disorders Usually First Diagnosed in Infancy, Childhood, or Adolescence contained in the *DSM-IV*, we have included selected disorders whose onset may or may not occur during childhood but whose manifestation is likely to concern school personnel.

Clinical Evaluations of School-Aged Children (2nd ed.) consists of three major inter-related components. One is a Checklist of 16 symptoms whose presence or absence should routinely be considered as part of the evaluation process. The second is an updated and revised Comprehensive Narrative of all characteristics for each disorder, including its associated features. The third is a revised Interview Form for use by mental health professionals when consulting with parents, teachers, and other school personnel.

The Checklist was designed to determine the presence or absence of such symptoms or behaviors as abnormal activity level, aggressiveness, anxiety, depression, inability to form or maintain social relationships, somatic complaints, hallucinations, delusions, language impairment, and impaired cognition, and the impact that a given syndrome may have on overall functioning. This Checklist will not by itself provide a comprehensive understanding of each disorder, but it may serve as an initial screening to consider or exclude any one diagnosis.

A Comprehensive Narrative of all characteristics is included for each of the disorders contained in this book. This section is vital in understanding a given syndrome. It includes all pertinent information and associated features and summarizes all the components that need to be considered to differentiate among a variety of syndromes. To ensure clarity, each description is based on the corresponding text found in the *DSM-IV.* It is presented in objective terms, allowing close comparison between the behaviors or symptoms of the referred child and those characteristics found in the Comprehensive Narrative.

The Interview Form* was developed to facilitate the gathering of information from different sources. It was specifically designed to follow diagnostic considerations and other environmental and familial factors outlined in the *DSM-IV.* It allows for an objective description of behaviors or symptoms and an expanded view of the child in a variety of settings.

Case Summaries have been included to illustrate the capacity of *Clinical Evaluations of School-Aged Children (2nd ed.)* to confirm a given diagnosis and to suggest areas that could be productively explored by those working with the child. Updated and new case illustrations have been added to conform to new diagnostic categories and changes in criteria of several disorders found in the *DSM-IV.* Cases included in this book were gathered from a diverse group of professionals, including psychiatrists, pediatricians, psychologists, social workers, and hospital, school, and private practitioners. Names and circumstances have been changed and modified to protect the confidentiality of specific individuals. Recommendations in the Case Summaries represent the opinions of the individual professionals and are not meant to be guidelines for treatment of the disorders included in this book.

To facilitate readers' understanding, the *Clinical Evaluations of School-Aged Children (2nd ed.)* contains several charts, such as a Summary Chart of Changes from the *DSM-III-R* to the *DSM-IV* (pp. xiii-xiv), a Mood Disorders Summary Chart (p. 117), and a Summary Checklist of Major Symptoms (pp. 329-331). In

---

* The binding of this book allows pages to lay flat for photocopying. You might wish to copy appropriate Interview Forms for use during your actual interviews. The publisher grants permission for you to photocopy solely for that purpose.

addition to updated references, a resource list of national associations for specific disorders is provided.

The reader is cautioned that many of the disorders described in the *DSM-IV* have questionable inter-rater reliability. Nonetheless, it is currently the most widely used reference manual among clinical practitioners. *Clinical Evaluations of School-Aged Children (2nd ed.)* has been developed primarily to assist mental health professionals in the organization and preparation of data. It does not replace the *DSM-IV* or the appropriate use of psychological testing, nor was it designed to provide a final clinical diagnosis.

We believe that the flexible design of *Clinical Evaluations of School-Aged Children (2nd ed.)* will enable mental health professionals to understand, organize, and expand on available information from a variety of perspectives. This should lead to clearer and more precise communication among the clinical practitioner, parents, and/or others working with the child in the school setting.

REFERENCES

American Psychiatric Association. (1987). *Diagnostic and Statistical Manual of Mental Disorders* (3rd ed. rev.). Washington, DC: Author.

American Psychiatric Association. (1994). *Diagnostic and Statistical Manual of Mental Disorders* (4th ed.). Washington, DC: Author.

Samuels, S. K., & Sikorsky, S. (1990). *Clinical Evaluations of School-Aged Children: A Structured Approach to the Diagnosis of Child and Adolescent Mental Disorders.* Sarasota, FL: Professional Resource Exchange, Inc.

Summary Chart of Changes
from the *DSM-III-R* to the *DSM-IV*

DISORDERS	NO	YES	COMMENTS
Attention-Deficit/Hyperactivity Disorder		X	Major changes in criteria - Three subtypes created
Adjustment Disorders (AD)		X	Regrouping of AD with Withdrawal, Physical Complaints, and Work or Academic Inhibition into one subtype named Adjustment Disorder, Unspecified Type Specifiers: Acute and Chronic
Anorexia Nervosa		X	Two subtypes created
Autistic Disorder	X		
Bipolar Disorders		X	Changes in subtypes
Bulimia Nervosa		X	Two subtypes created
Chronic Motor and Vocal Tic Disorder		X	Duration
Conduct Disorder		X	Regrouping into two types. New criteria added
Cyclothymic Disorder	X		
Dream Anxiety Disorder		X	Name changed to Nightmare Disorder
Dysthymic Disorder	X		
Elective Mutism		X	Name changed to Selective Mutism. Duration; exclusionary criteria added
Encopresis		X	Two subtypes created. Duration
Enuresis		X	Three subtypes created. Frequency and duration
Gender Identity Disorder		X	Minimum changes
Hypomanic Episode		X	Duration; criteria changed
Identity Disorder		X	Moved to "Other Conditions" section of *DSM-IV*

Summary Chart of Changes
from the *DSM-III-R* to the *DSM-IV* (Cont'd)

DISORDERS	NO	YES	COMMENTS
Major Depressive Disorder	X		
Major Depressive Episode		X	Some criteria changed
Manic Episode		X	Duration
Obsessive-Compulsive Disorder		X	Some exclusionary criteria
Oppositional Defiant Disorder		X	Minor changes in criteria
Overanxious Disorder of Childhood	X		Incorporated into Generalized Anxiety Disorder
Pica		X	Criteria for developmental level
Posttraumatic Stress Disorder	X		
Reactive Attachment Disorder		X	Two subtypes created
Rumination Disorder		X	Criteria concerning weight loss deleted
Separation Anxiety Disorder	X		
Sleep Terror Disorder	X		
Sleepwalking Disorder	X		
Social Phobia		X	Minor clarifications in criteria
Tourette's Disorder		X	Duration
Transient Tic Disorder		X	Significant changes in criteria for diagnosis

NEW DISORDERS IN THE *DSM-IV*

Asperger's Disorder
Childhood Disintegrative Disorder

Feeding Disorder of Infancy or Early Childhood
Rett's Disorder

CLINICAL EVALUATIONS OF SCHOOL-AGED CHILDREN

A Structured Approach to the Diagnosis of Child and Adolescent Mental Disorders

Second Edition

DISRUPTIVE BEHAVIOR DISORDERS

ATTENTION-DEFICIT/ HYPERACTIVITY DISORDER

The *DSM-III-R* previously described Attention-Deficit/ Hyperactivity Disorder as a unified syndrome characterized by behaviors of inattention, impulsiveness, and hyperactivity. The *DSM-IV* establishes three subtypes of the disorder: Attention-Deficit/Hyperactivity Disorder, Predominantly Inattentive Type; Attention-Deficit/Hyperactivity Disorder, Predominantly Hyperactive-Impulsive Type; and Attention-Deficit/Hyperactivity Disorder, Combined Type. In addition, the *DSM-IV* requires that the behaviors associated with Attention-Deficit/Hyperactivity Disorder be present in more than one setting (i.e., school and home).

♦ **Attention-Deficit/Hyperactivity Disorder, Predominantly Inattentive Type:** This classification is given when the behaviors present are primarily associated with inattention, with few or no hyperactive or impulsive behaviors consistently noted.

Inattention in a child with Attention-Deficit/Hyperactivity Disorder may be manifested by poor listening skills, inability to complete tasks or organize work, or other activities. Children with this disorder have difficulty sustaining attention and are easily distracted by peripheral stimuli. They tend to miss essential details, may be careless in their schoolwork, may be forgetful with daily responsibilities, and often lose the tools and materials necessary for work or play. Because these children have such difficulty staying focused on a task, they often tend to avoid activities which require concentrated mental effort. Such difficulties with attention also manifest themselves in the child's social interactions. For example, he or she may have difficulties following a conversation, staying on a topic, picking up subtle social cues, and maintaining the rules of a game once it has started.

♦ **Attention-Deficit/Hyperactivity Disorder, Predominantly Hyperactive-Impulsive Type:** This diagnosis is given when the behaviors present are primarily associated with hyperactivity and impulsivity. Inattention may still be present in this subtype but to a lesser degree than in the Predominantly Inattentive Type.

Hyperactivity is often characterized by restlessness, fidgeting, excessive running, endless talking, and inability to sit still for an age-appropriate length of time. The lack of goal-directed, organized motor activity differentiates this disorder from ordinary overactivity. The level of hyperactivity varies with the child, his or her age, and the structural organization of the environment. For example, the child's behavior may be appropriate in a new, one-to-one, or small group situation but might become disorganized in a large group setting. Different degrees of hyperactivity may be seen in school during such times as lunch, independent work periods, recess, or in teacher-directed lessons. At home or when engaged in leisure activities, these children are often excessively noisy, frequently shifting from one activity to another. In adolescence, overt gross motor activity tends to be less obvious and may be replaced by feelings of agitation and restlessness.

Impulsivity may be noted in children with this disorder by their difficulty in taking turns, their tendency to act before thinking, and their constant invasions into someone else's space. They often interrupt or intrude upon others who are engaged in work or social activities. These children also tend to be accident prone because of carelessness, and generally require ongoing adult intervention and supervision.

♦ **Attention-Deficit/Hyperactivity Disorder, Combined Type:** This is the most frequently diagnosed type of Attention-Deficit/Hyperactivity Disorder. Behaviors of inattention and hyperactivity/impulsivity are present to a significant degree. This type may be preceded by either the Predominantly Inattentive Type or Hyperactive-Impulsive Type.

Regardless of the subtype of this disorder, children diagnosed with Attention-Deficit/Hyperactivity Disorder may experience low self-esteem and difficulty with interpersonal relationships. Attitudes and behaviors may also include mood swings, low frustration tolerance, temper tantrums, bossiness, negativism, obstinacy, and poor responses to authority. Conflicts within the family or at school are common because these children are sometimes perceived as lazy, stubborn, unmotivated, or noncompliant. Children with Attention-Deficit/Hyperactivity Disorder are at risk for developing Oppositional Defiant Disorder and Conduct Disorder and are more likely to experience school failure. Children with this disorder tend to come from families with a history of Attention-Deficit/Hyperactivity Disorder.

The need to obtain information from multiple sources and settings is crucial to an accurate diagnosis. Behaviors such as inattention, impulsivity, excessive motor activity, and lack of goal directedness may be symptomatic of a chaotic environmental background, child abuse, understimulation, or health-related conditions rather than indicative of an Attention-Deficit Disorder.

The practitioner is cautioned that diagnosis of Attention-Deficit/Hyperactivity Disorder is a complex endeavor. It is especially difficult to diagnose in preschool children because of their normally high activity levels, natural curiosity, and desire to explore their environment. In school-aged children, misdiagnosis may occur as a result of the mismatch between the child's intellectual ability and the demands of the classroom. This discrepancy may cause the child to show behaviors of Attention-Deficit/Hyperactivity Disorder (i.e., inattention, restlessness, lack of work completion). However, this does not necessarily preclude the existence of this disorder in a given child; for example, gifted and/or mentally retarded children may also suffer from Attention-Deficit/Hyperactivity Disorder.

Table of Contents for Attention-Deficit/Hyperactivity Disorder

☑ CHECKLIST

ATTENTION-DEFICIT/ HYPERACTIVITY DISORDER

KEY	+	Presence
	-	Absence
	*	Associated Feature

MAJOR SYMPTOMS:

+	Inattention
+	Impulsivity
+	Abnormal Activity Level
-	Aggressiveness
-	Violation of Rules
-	Isolation/Withdrawal/Avoidance
*	Inability to Form/Maintain Relationships
-	Disturbances of Affect/Mood
-	Anxiety
-	Depression
-	Delusions/Hallucinations
-	Somatic Complaints
-	Oddities of Behavior
-	Language Impairment
-	Impaired Cognition
+	Significant Distress/Impairment in Important Areas of Functioning

INTERVIEW FORM
ATTENTION-DEFICIT/ HYPERACTIVITY DISORDER

1. Is the child easily distracted by surrounding noises or people?
   ☐ Yes ☐ No

2. Does the child often fail to finish things he or she starts?
   ☐ Yes ☐ No

3. Is the child able to sustain attention in schoolwork or play activities?   ☐ Yes ☐ No

4. Does the child frequently make careless errors in homework or classwork?   ☐ Yes ☐ No

5. Does the child often appear not to listen?
   ☐ Yes ☐ No

6. Does the child have difficulties organizing himself or herself, such as losing pencils, books, or toys in school or at home?
   ☐ Yes ☐ No

7. Does the child fidget excessively (in younger children, squirming in seat; in adolescents, feelings of restlessness)?
   ☐ Yes ☐ No

8. Does the child have difficulty remaining seated when required to do so?   ☐ Yes ☐ No

9. Does the child have difficulty waiting his or her turn in games or group situations?   ☐ Yes ☐ No

10. Does the child blurt out answers to questions before they have been completed?   ☐ Yes ☐ No

11. Does the child often and unintentionally shift from one uncompleted activity to another?   ☐ Yes ☐ No

12. Does the child have difficulty playing and/or working quietly?   ☐ Yes ☐ No

13. Does the child often talk incessantly as though his or her mind is going "a mile a minute"?   ☐ Yes ☐ No

14. Does the child often interrupt or encroach on the activities of others?   ☐ Yes ☐ No

15. Does the child engage in reckless or physically harmful activities without considering the consequences?
☐ Yes ☐ No   Describe.

16. Does the child display low frustration tolerance?
☐ Yes ☐ No

17. Are the child's interpersonal relationships negatively affected by his or her behaviors?   ☐ Yes ☐ No   Describe.

18. What are the child's responses to disciplinary attempts? Describe.

19. Are the expectations for the child appropriate to his or her age and developmental levels?   ☐ Yes ☐ No

20. At what age and for how long have behaviors associated with inattention and/or impulsivity/hyperactivity been noticed? Describe.

21. Is there a history of significant environmental factors, such as chaotic home conditions, child abuse, understimulation, and/or health concerns?   ☐ Yes ☐ No   Describe.

CASE SUMMARY
ATTENTION-DEFICIT/
HYPERACTIVITY DISORDER
Andy, C.A. 4–10

Reason for Referral: Andy, a preschool child, was referred for evaluation because of concerns about his behavior. He was extremely active, distractible, and oppositional. Because of his behavior, Andy was dismissed from a nursery school program. Although active most of the time, Andy could reportedly sit for as long as 30 minutes, either watching television or playing with his Legos.

Consultant's Report: For the first 15 minutes of the session, Andy constantly tried to get out of his seat. The psychologist had to hold Andy's chair next to the table, but even with those restraints, he was out of the seat several times.

The most noticeable factors influencing Andy's intelligence test scores were his inability to concentrate and respond to verbal directions. When asked a question, his answers were barely related. For instance, when shown a thumb and asked to name it, he answered "mouth"; when asked what lives in water, he answered "water in the sink, clean the dishes." It was unclear whether Andy misunderstood the question, was not able to comprehend the words, or was too distracted to hear the complete question.

In summary, Andy was an active 4-year-old who demonstrated distractible behaviors. Although he was seen for three sessions, Andy was unable to attend long enough to allow a valid estimate of his intellectual potential. The major recommendation was for Andy's parents to address the issue of behavior management.

Psychiatric Consultation: Andy was recently removed from a local nursery school. Both his teacher and parents feel that Andy will not be able to function in a regular kindergarten. He obeys the teacher but is very active and distractible. His attention span is about 60 to 90 seconds. He talks endlessly, jumping from one subject to another, and it is difficult to follow what he is saying. Andy learns better on a one-to-one basis, but he can't seem to grasp some things. He is significantly low on readiness skills, has a low frustration tolerance, and may cry if he can't get his way. Andy is bossy and manipulative with peers. They seem to tolerate him and play alongside him, but real friendship is questionable.

Andy's activity level is consistently very high. He frequently shifts his attention and interest. His performance on tests of fine motor coordination is poor. There is a strong indication that Andy is experiencing an Attention Deficit/Hyperactivity Disorder with severe impairment, attested by failure in school, inability to be managed at home, and poor peer relationships. Stimulant medication may be necessary and some behaviorally oriented psychotherapy will almost certainly be needed. In school, I recommend a highly structured, self-contained classroom.

AUTHORS' COMMENTS: Andy manifests many of the symptoms associated with Attention-Deficit/Hyperactivity Disorder, Predominantly Hyperactive-Impulsive Type. He is unable to follow directions, is highly distractible, and is unable to concentrate on age-appropriate tasks. Andy's excessive activity levels further illustrate the presence of this disorder.

Andy also displays several additional features associated with Attention-Deficit/Hyperactivity Disorder, such as bossiness, oppositional tendencies, manipulative behaviors, and poor school performance, as evidenced by his dismissal from nursery school and his low readiness skills.

CASE SUMMARY
ATTENTION-DEFICIT/ HYPERACTIVITY DISORDER
Tyrone, C.A. 8–5

Reason for Referral: Tyrone was referred by his pediatrician because of an increasing pattern of impulsivity and distractibility. An Attention-Deficit/Hyperactivity Disorder assessment was performed as part of a full psychoeducational evaluation.

Assessment Instruments: Interviews with Tyrone's parents, Conners' Continuous Performance Test, Attention-Deficit/ Hyperactivity Disorder Rating Scale, Achenbach Child Behavior Checklist, and Achenbach Teacher Report Form.

Relevant History: Tyrone had demonstrated a pattern of impulsivity and distractibility since age 4. His father has a number of Attention-Deficit/Hyperactivity Disorder symptoms. There are significant family tensions at home.

Results: The Attention-Deficit/Hyperactivity Disorder Rating Scale completed by Tyrone's teacher was notable in that all questions were endorsed as "very much," which is the highest level of severity for the items. Separate Attention-Deficit/Hyperactivity Disorder Rating Scales were filled out by Tyrone's parents, where a high number of items were endorsed as "pretty much." On the Teacher Report Form, Tyrone fell in the clinically significant range on the Attention Problems Scale, the Aggressive Behavior Scale, and the Social Problems Scale. On the Child Behavior Checklist, the parents' responses resulted in Tyrone's scoring in the clinically significant range on the Aggressive and Delinquent Behavior Scales. On both forms, the Attention Problems Scale was particularly elevated. On the Continuous Performance Test, Tyrone quickly became bored and refused to continue with it. His teachers report that he generally insists on high-energy activities (such as playing catch). He tests limits frequently and may become quite angry if the teacher points out a rule or limit.

Conclusion and Recommendations: Tyrone manifests numerous symptoms of Attention-Deficit/Hyperactivity Disorder, including impulsivity, inattention, and hyperactivity.   It is felt that a trial of medication is warranted.   In addition, Tyrone would require a good deal of structure at school in order to internalize rules of behavior.   He would likely benefit from a positively geared behavioral system which would reward constructive behaviors.

AUTHORS' COMMENTS: This case is part of a comprehensive psychological evaluation.   It was chosen to illustrate the use of behavior rating scales in the process of diagnosing Attention-Deficit/Hyperactivity Disorder.   Following best practices, the evaluator should use multiple sources to gather behavioral information and determine the presence of pathology according to normative methods.

CONDUCT DISORDER

The *DSM-III-R* included three types of Conduct Disorder: Solitary Aggressive Type, Group Type, and Undifferentiated Type. In the *DSM-IV,* only two types of Conduct Disorder are described: Childhood-Onset Type and Adolescent-Onset Type. In both subtypes, the violation of basic rights and societal norms is divided into four distinct patterns of behavior: Aggression towards people and animals, Destruction of property, Deceitfulness or theft, and Serious violation of rules.

The major characteristic of Conduct Disorder is a long-term, recurrent pattern of behaviors that violates the basic rights of others or major age-appropriate societal rules and norms. The seriousness of such behaviors differentiates this disorder from the common mischief and antics of children and adolescents and results in impaired functioning in social, academic, or occupational settings.

♦ **Childhood-Onset Type:** This type of Conduct Disorder pertains to children before age 10, who exhibit behaviors such as physical aggression, poor peer relationships, or oppositional tendencies. It is more commonly diagnosed among males. By puberty, these children are likely to display at least one of the more serious behaviors pertaining to the four categories outlined previously. In adulthood, they are more likely to develop Antisocial Personality Disorder than those who have been diagnosed with Adolescent-Onset Conduct Disorder.

♦ **Adolescent-Onset Type:** Unlike the Childhood-Onset Type, children diagnosed with this type of Conduct Disorder do not display any of the characteristics associated with the disorder before the age of 10. They tend to have better peer relationships and show less aggression towards others. As adults, they are less likely to develop into individuals with Antisocial Personality Disorder.

The characteristics associated with each of the four patterns of behavior in Conduct Disorder are as follows:

1. In the *Aggression towards people and animals,* the child is reported as threatening, intimidating, bullying others, and

starting physical fights. He or she may have engaged in acts of cruelty towards people or animals, and/or forced sexual activity on others. Weapons may be used in confrontations when engaged in robbery and/or assault.

2. ***Destruction of property*** includes behaviors which are intended to cause serious damage, such as fire-setting or using explosives.

3. ***Deceitfulness or theft*** involves breaking and entering, lying or manipulating others for gain, or stealing items of significant value.

4. ***Serious violation of rules*** includes such behaviors as truancy from school, staying out at night, and running away from home.

Children with Conduct Disorder show a prolonged pattern of behavioral difficulties at home, in school, and in the community. Precocious sexual activity, substance abuse at an early age, and other reckless behaviors are often present. Sexually transmitted diseases and unplanned pregnancies may result. Low self-esteem is usually masked by an air of toughness. Because these children tend to misinterpret behaviors of others as menacing, they will respond in an aggressive manner and may initiate fights or assaults. Thus, the rate of physical injury experienced by children and adolescents with this disorder can be higher than in the normal population. In general, males tend to engage in more confrontational, aggressive behaviors than females, who are likely to exhibit more covert, manipulative, or self-destructive behaviors.

In school, children with Conduct Disorder tend to be underachievers, inattentive, and often display low verbal skills and reading difficulties. At home and in school they show irritability, temper tantrums, and poor frustration tolerance. Incidents of suicidal gestures, attempts, and completions may be present at a higher rate.

Common in this disorder is a tendency to manipulate others for advantage and lack of guilt or remorse. When caught or confronted, these children appear unable to accept responsibility for their behavior, and tend to accuse and blame others. If they acknowledge responsibility for their behavior, it is only to avoid negative consequences. In general, they do not express concern for the feelings, wishes, or well-being of others, and are perceived by others as inconsiderate and self-centered.

Children are more at risk of developing Conduct Disorder if there is a familial history of Antisocial Personality Disorder, Conduct Disorder, Attention-Deficit Disorder, or Substance Abuse. Other risk factors in the child's life include poor parenting skills, physical and/or sexual abuse, absence of parental figures, rejection or instability in the home environment, and association with delinquent groups.

Because of a tendency to overdiagnose Conduct Disorder in children from violence-ridden environments, the practitioner must consider the child's behaviors within the context of his or her social setting. If such behaviors are considered as reactive, defensive, and necessary for survival, a diagnosis of Conduct Disorder may not necessarily apply.

Table of Contents for
Conduct Disorder

☑ CHECKLIST
CONDUCT DISORDER

```
        +  Presence
KEY     -  Absence
        *  Associated
           Feature
```

MAJOR SYMPTOMS:

*	Inattention
*	Impulsivity
-	Abnormal Activity Level
+	Aggressiveness
+	Violation of Rules
-	Isolation/Withdrawal/Avoidance
-	Inability to Form/Maintain Relationships
*	Disturbances of Affect/Mood
-	Anxiety
-	Depression
-	Delusions/Hallucinations
-	Somatic Complaints
-	Oddities of Behavior
-	Language Impairment
-	Impaired Cognition
+	Significant Distress/Impairment in Important Areas of Functioning

INTERVIEW FORM
CONDUCT DISORDER

1. Does the child exhibit evidence of physical violence against persons or property?   ☐ Yes ☐ No

2. Has the child been physically cruel towards people?
    ☐ Yes ☐ No

3. Does the child engage in physical cruelty towards animals?
    ☐ Yes ☐ No

4. Has the child forced someone into sexual activity?
    ☐ Yes ☐ No

5. Has the child used a weapon during a confrontation?
    ☐ Yes ☐ No

6. Has the child committed thefts involving confrontation with the victim, such as extortion, purse snatching, or armed robbery?   ☐ Yes ☐ No

7. Has the child deliberately engaged in fire-setting or other destruction of property?   ☐ Yes ☐ No

8. Has the child been involved in stealing surreptitiously without confronting the victim?   ☐ Yes ☐ No

9. Is the child a persistent and serious liar?   ☐ Yes ☐ No

10. Has the child engaged in breaking and entering?
    ☐ Yes ☐ No

11. Has the child repeatedly run away from home?
    ☐ Yes ☐ No

12. Is the child persistently truant from school?
    ☐ Yes ☐ No

13. Is the child able to express genuine guilt or remorse for his or her actions?   ☐ Yes ☐ No

14. Does the child avoid blaming or informing on others?
    ☐ Yes ☐ No

15. Does the child show care and concern for the welfare of others?   ☐ Yes ☐ No

16. What is the child's achievement in school compared to his or her learning potential? Describe.

17. Has the child used or abused illegal substances?
    ☐ Yes ☐ No

18. Does the child exhibit symptoms of an Attention-Deficit/ Hyperactivity Disorder?   ☐ Yes ☐ No

19. At what age did the child first manifest behaviors associated with Conduct Disorder?

CASE SUMMARY
CONDUCT DISORDER: CHILDHOOD-ONSET TYPE
Luis, C.A. 15–4

Reason for Referral: Luis is a 15-year-old referred by the school because of long-term concerns about his behavior and academic performance. Since the end of 2nd grade when Luis was 7½, his primary exceptionality has been Social and Emotional Maladjustment. Longstanding behaviors such as fighting, disruption, swearing, and antagonism have been reported. He has also been known to Juvenile Court for shoplifting and vandalism.

Background Information: On the psychological evaluation, Luis' intellectual performance on the WISC-III placed him in the bright average range of intellectual functioning. There was a large disparity between his Verbal and Performance scores, resulting in his Verbal IQ being in the Low Average range, whereas his Performance IQ was in the Superior range.

Luis, at one time, was engaged in fecal soiling. He does have a history of seizures for which he has taken Dilantin for some period of time. A referral to Protective Services was made 2 years ago when Luis was reported beyond control and because he had engaged in runaway behaviors.

Mother reports that while she is away at work, Luis brings acquaintances home. Since they smoke a great deal, she is fearful that he will start a fire in the house. They use "dirty language" and smoke marijuana and drink. At times, Luis stays out all night. Mother also stated that her husband, from whom she is separated, and Luis are often in conflict with each other. In contrast to Luis, his father gets along with his other two sons.

Luis arrived at the interview accompanied by the school psychologist. He entered the interview room readily and without noticeable signs of anxiety. Discussing his schoolwork, Luis commented that it was a "normal routine" and "no big deal." It was apparent that he was quite evasive and wished to avoid disclosure of school-related problems. When questioned about this school year's grades, Luis stated that the teachers "gave him" four F's. The evaluator found it necessary to extract information piece by piece. Luis disclosed that he was in a special program. Further, he was suspended several times for breaking a school window, fighting, and disruptive behavior.

Diagnosis: Conduct Disorder: Childhood-Onset Type

Recommendations:

1. Placement in a residential center of a highly structured type with a policy of firm limit-setting. It is advisable that his parents become involved in family-oriented psychotherapy while Luis resides in the placement center.
2. Since Luis refuses to take responsibility for his actions, it is important that limit-setting be clear and definite with immediate and specific consequences for his negative behaviors.

AUTHORS' COMMENTS: In the Childhood-Onset Type, the child presents a long-term pattern of physical aggressiveness, increasingly serious violation of rules, and poor interpersonal relationships. Luis is seen as a self-centered youngster who has been out of control at home and school since the 2nd grade. At present, this is evidenced by his truancy, frequent suspensions for fighting, attempts to run away, smoking marijuana, drinking, theft, and vandalism. Although he associates with others, these relationships appear to be superficial at best and centered around illegal activities. The disruptive behaviors seem to be initiated by Luis and carried out on his own.

In addition, Luis' encopresis until age 11 may be viewed as further evidence of emotional difficulties. Because of his behavior, he has been unable to achieve in school despite his good intellectual potential. The severity of Luis' conduct warranted removal from the mainstream and placement in an institutional setting.

CASE SUMMARY

CONDUCT DISORDER: ADOLESCENT-ONSET TYPE
Charles, C.A. 13–0

Reason for Referral: Charles, chronologically a 7th grader, has experienced significant difficulties this year and last year in work completion, interpersonal relationships, and appropriate school behavior. He is often absent from school and exhibits little concern about completing work. He takes no responsibility for his actions and is very creative in his use of excuses, sometimes becoming oppositional and disrespectful towards adults. Behavior on the bus is a problem. Recently, Charles punched another child in the face and was suspended for 4 days.

Charles has received direct service in the Learning Center due to a Learning Disability. He currently functions below customary 7th grade academic expectations. He has spotty skill development with some mastery at the 4th, 5th, and 6th grade levels. School reports reflect a history of task avoidance, lack of motivation in the school setting, and a defiant attitude.

Charles lives with his mother and two older brothers. Mother currently works two jobs. His parents are divorced and his father has maintained some contact with the children over the years.

School Psychologist's Findings and Recommendations: Charles was not spontaneous in conversation. He had many reasons for his difficulties in school, such as "Don't understand the directions," and "Just being lazy." He also had excuses for not doing homework and for being late. Charles told the examiner about shooting cows in the rear with his BB gun, commenting that he likes to see them jump and make noise. He responded to the formal testing rather passively, often leaning on his elbow and delivering his responses in a flat tone.

Projective testing and observations of behavior reveal Charles to be immature, angry, still at odds with authority, and unsuccessful at controlling his impulses. The stories that Charles related in response to the TAT cards contained people who were passive, unmotivated, and nonaccepting of responsibility. Evident throughout the testing were Charles' oppositional tendencies.

Significant hostility and a hypercritical attitude towards others obstruct empathetic relations and interfere with an appropriately developing value system.

Psychiatric Consultation: Charles came to the interview willingly. He related rather coldly and callously at first but was able to respond more appropriately when effectively confronted. His affect was appropriate to his mood. Charles' mentation was clear in most areas with the outstanding exception of his thoughts about authority. He attempted to use a variety of verbal manipulations when questioned about this issue. When these failed, he finally and reluctantly admitted that he fails to acknowledge the authority of school personnel when he feels like it.

If this pattern were to continue, it could lead to the development of an Antisocial Personality Disorder. I recommend a high degree of structure in the school environment. He seems to confuse authority with freedom of thought. It is important that he learn to distinguish between those two factors. To that end, Charles' mother agreed to intercede on behalf of school personnel whenever Charles violates school rules.

Diagnosis: Conduct Disorder: Adolescent-Onset Type

AUTHORS' COMMENTS: Charles' behavior has deteriorated since the onset of early adolescence and is manifested now by overt aggression, some instances of assault to peers, cruelty to animals, and difficulties with school-related tasks. These behaviors constitute a significant violation of the basic rights of others and of general societal rules. In addition, there is a lack of empathy towards the well-being of others. Background history also reveals inconsistent limit-setting and intermittent presence of parental figures. At present, Charles' behaviors meet the minimum criteria for diagnosis of Conduct Disorder: Adolescent-Onset Type.

CASE SUMMARY

CONDUCT DISORDER: ATTENTION-DEFICIT/ HYPERACTIVITY DISORDER, AND IMPULSE CONTROL DISORDER
Ted, C.A. 14–0

Presenting Problem: This is the first psychiatric admission for this 14-year-old male who lives with his mother, stepfather, and brother. He was recently arrested for breaking and entering his school and breaking windows, stealing a camera, and killing fish. He also stole a report from the school about himself and burned it at home. He has a history of breaking and entering into homes but has not always been caught. Ted has been arrested approximately five times. He says he "likes the thrill of it and adrenaline rush just before getting caught." Ted is currently on medication for Attention-Deficit Disorder, but he claims that the medication is not as effective as it has been in the past. He has been extremely impulsive and out of control. Although not present at this time, there is a history of sadness with some fleeting suicidal ideation. During the first part of last year Ted lived with his father, who allegedly is a recovering alcoholic and is involved in drug sales. His brother has been involved with gangs and was arrested for selling drugs. The school had Ted on homebound tutoring, but the teacher was afraid to go to his home. The first part of last year, when Ted lived with his father, he didn't go to school at all. He finally returned to live with his mother. Ted states that he smokes marijuana once every couple of weeks, and has drunk alcohol several times in the last few months, one time getting drunk. He has had many fights with his friends and has had problems with lying and destruction of property. Ted has had sleep disturbances and anxiety although no panic attacks.

Mental Status: Ted is a well-developed, well-nourished adolescent male, appearing younger than his stated age of 14. He was cooperative throughout the interview. Speech was goal directed and no psychomotor dysfunction was noted. Mood was slightly depressed but affect was appropriate. Ted stated that he occasionally has difficulty falling asleep and can stay awake until 2:00 or 3:00 in the morning. He has difficulty getting up during the day. He states that he eats when he is bored and feels that, "Life is a big bore. I am trying to have fun all the time, which is how I get into trouble." He allegedly has gained 25 pounds in the last year, but this may be due to a growth spurt, as he does not appear at all heavy. Ted denies anhedonia although his boredom may in fact be anhedonia. He denies anergia and states that occasionally he has some guilty feelings although not often. He has difficulty concentrating. Ted denies libidinal complaints, somatic problems, or suicidal ideation although he stated that he used to wish he had never been born. He denies homicidal ideation although he gets into many arguments and fist fights. He is also verbally abusive. Ted denies hallucinations and delusions, and there is no evidence of a thought disorder. Although he denies panic attacks, phobias, or obsessions, he does admit to some anxiety. There is a history of fire-setting. When Ted was about 10 years old, he set the woods on fire but was able to put it out.

Diagnosis: Ted has a history of Attention-Deficit/ Hyperactivity Disorder with poor frustration tolerance and distractibility, inattentiveness, and high levels of impulsivity. His impulse control is so poor that he says that what comes into his head is what he does. His behaviors have become so disruptive that the authorities have been involved on numerous occasions. Ted currently fits the criteria for Conduct Disorder: Attention-Deficit/Hyperactivity Disorder, Impulse Control Disorder.

AUTHORS' COMMENTS: Ted has been out of control at home, in school, and in the community and has been arrested several times for violation of major societal rules. He has been aggressive towards peers and adults, has harmed animals, has stolen and destroyed property, has been truant from school, and has engaged in fire-setting. Although he has a severe Conduct Disorder, it is unclear from the report if the onset of the behaviors described earlier occurred before age 10.

Ted has a history of Attention-Deficit/Hyperactivity Disorder and although he is on medication, he displays significant and ongoing problems with impulse control; this would warrant an additional diagnosis of Impulse Control Disorder. Ted reported a history of sadness, boredom, and fleeting suicidal ideation. The presence of Dysthymic Disorder or other depressive features could have been further explored.

OPPOSITIONAL
DEFIANT DISORDER

Oppositional Defiant Disorder in the *DSM-IV* essentially follows the same diagnostic criteria as the *DSM-III-R*. The disorder is characterized by a persistent antagonistic attitude, especially towards authority figures such as parents and teachers, past the developmental age when oppositional behaviors frequently occur (18 to 36 months of age). Behaviors such as negativism, swearing, provocativeness, disobedience, stubbornness, argumentativeness, procrastination, and passive resistance are common, even when they are obviously against the self-interest and well-being of the child or adolescent.

Most often the individual sees others as the cause of his or her difficulties; he or she is unable to assume responsibility and views others as demanding and essentially unreasonable. Frequent behaviors include violations of minor rules, opposition to any suggestions, refusal to follow directions, and inability to refrain from carrying out an act which has been specifically forbidden. School and family difficulties are commonly associated with this disorder. Social relationships may be affected because of the hostile, oppositional attitude exhibited by these children even when engaged in pleasurable peer activities. There may also be use of substances, such as tobacco, alcohol, and cannabis.

This overall pattern of confrontation is generally more upsetting and disruptive to the adults than to the child. Oppositional behaviors are more common with people who are familiar to the child; thus, these behaviors may not be evident during formal evaluation in a clinical setting. It may be necessary to gather specific data from sources familiar with the child rather than base a diagnosis solely on the clinical assessment. In addition, because negativistic behaviors tend to be prevalent among preschool-age children and adolescents, the practitioner should use caution when considering a child to have Oppositional Defiant Disorder during those stages of development.

In general, males tend to exhibit more confrontational and prolonged symptoms than females. In many cases, Oppositional Defiant Disorder precedes the development of a Conduct Disorder. Oppositional Defiant Disorder appears to be more prevalent in families with a history of Mood Disorders, Oppositional Defiant Disorder, Conduct Disorder, Attention-Deficit

Disorder, Antisocial Personality Disorder, and Substance Abuse. Poor parenting skills and frequent change in caregivers may also place a child at risk for developing this disorder.

All the features of the Oppositional Defiant Disorder may be present in the Conduct Disorder. The latter involves violations of major rules and basic rights of others. For this reason, diagnosis of Conduct Disorder would preempt a diagnosis of Oppositional Defiant Disorder. In some cases, Attention-Deficit Disorder may also be present, warranting an additional diagnosis.

Table of Contents for
Oppositional Defiant Disorder

☑ CHECKLIST

OPPOSITIONAL
DEFIANT DISORDER

	+	**Presence**
KEY	**-**	**Absence**
	*	**Associated Feature**

MAJOR SYMPTOMS:

-	Inattention
-	Impulsivity
-	Abnormal Activity Level
+	Aggressiveness
*	Violation of Rules
-	Isolation/Withdrawal/Avoidance
*	Inability to Form/Maintain Relationships
-	Disturbances of Affect/Mood
-	Anxiety
-	Depression
-	Delusions/Hallucinations
-	Somatic Complaints
-	Oddities of Behavior
-	Language Impairment
-	Impaired Cognition
+	Significant Distress/Impairment in Important Areas of Functioning

INTERVIEW FORM

OPPOSITIONAL
DEFIANT DISORDER

1. Does the child often lose his or her temper?
    ☐ Yes ☐ No

2. Does the child often argue with adults? ☐ Yes ☐ No

3. Does the child often blatantly refuse to comply with adult
    requests or rules? ☐ Yes ☐ No

4. Does the child purposely engage in behaviors to annoy
    others? ☐ Yes ☐ No

5. Does the child usually blame others for his or her difficulties?
    ☐ Yes ☐ No

6. Does the child appear overly sensitive and easily annoyed
    by others? ☐ Yes ☐ No

7. Does the child often appear angry and resentful?
    ☐ Yes ☐ No

8. Is the child reported to be vindictive or spiteful?
    ☐ Yes ☐ No

9. Does the child often swear and use obscenities?
    ☐ Yes ☐ No

10. Do such behaviors persist even when positive reinforcements
    are offered, such as concrete rewards, adult attention, or
    good grades? ☐ Yes ☐ No

11. To what extent is the family and/or school affected by the
    child's behavior? Describe.

12.   To what extent are the child's peer relationships affected by his or her oppositional behavior? Describe.

13.   Are these oppositional behaviors severe enough to include violation of major rules and basic rights of others (e.g., theft, vandalism, physical aggression, persistent truancy, and drug abuse)?   ☐ Yes ☐ No

CASE SUMMARY

OPPOSITIONAL DEFIANT DISORDER
Abe, C.A. 14–0

Reason for Referral: Abe was referred for evaluation because of behavior problems in school and at home, and poor relationships with family members. He is reported to be an angry, argumentative youngster, often refusing to comply with simple parental requests. At school, Abe teases other children, and when confronted about his behavior, he quickly blames his peers. His use of obscene language has warranted removal from class and several suspensions.

Consultant's Report: Abe demonstrates considerable immaturity. There is out-of-control behavior of an aggressive and oppositional nature, and a great deal of resentment towards his younger brother. This resentment was recently displayed by two incidents: one in which he threw sand into his brother's eyes and another in which he threw ammonia into his brother's eyes. Both of these were treated as accidents by mother, suggesting denial and poor ability on her part to generate control over his behavior.

Abe also has a tendency to be extremely manipulative and to make excuses for his behaviors, indicating that they are caused by other people. He has an extremely low frustration tolerance and is virtually unwilling to do anything that appears work-like in school. In this instance, the diagnosis is Oppositional Defiant Disorder.

Recommendations:

1. Without intervention, Abe is seriously at risk for developing a Conduct Disorder. Therefore, it is recommended that Abe see a counselor with his mother to establish behavioral controls and to support his mother through the resentment and acting-out behavior that is likely to occur during the establishment of these behavioral controls.

2. The school should consider placement in a special class for behaviorally disordered children.

AUTHOR'S COMMENTS: Abe's oppositional behaviors, as characterized by his resistance to schoolwork and provocative attitude at school and towards his family members, are two patterns found in Oppositional Defiant Disorder. In addition, Abe frequently confronts his mother to the point where she can no longer control him.

Abe's aggressive acts are potentially dangerous to his brother and thus could be construed as the beginning stages of a Conduct Disorder.

It is important to determine what Abe's response to behavioral modification techniques has been thus far because very often these children do not respond well to positive reinforcement.

Another common feature of children with this disorder is poor peer relationships because of a pervasive antagonistic attitude, even when engaged in play activities. Therefore, the evaluation should have included some specificity regarding Abe's interactions with peers.

CASE SUMMARY

OPPOSITIONAL DEFIANT DISORDER
Peter, C.A. 15–7

Reason for Referral: A psychiatric consultation was requested for Peter because episodically he assumes the role of another person. For example, he will mimic a teacher and carry out that person's role for a few minutes at which point he may stop and sit down in his seat. While in the school psychologist's office he pretends to be a given teacher, indicating he is no longer a student, and as the teacher, he will chastise another student or will take on the characteristics of the personality whose role he's assuming and in the course of his role playing may get genuinely angry.

In written themes, Peter provides content that is filled with gory details involving murders, dismembering bodies, and demons, as well as sexual themes of exploring, or having sexual contact with girls.

When with the school psychologist, Peter may commit himself to an academic task, but gives up easily and invariably fails. At that point he becomes very self-critical and while in that state, he may cry.

At home, Peter stares out the window and talks to himself, or he will stand in his underwear and pretend he is playing his guitar as if he were a rock singer. At times, he becomes angry and swears under his breath. At other times, he mocks his parents and jabbers to himself making such sarcastic comments as, "You are so smart." He has stolen money from his parents and has run up outrageous long-distance telephone bills.

The aforementioned behaviors have been continuous throughout elementary school but are getting worse. When Peter was in nursery school, his parents were alerted to difficulties he was experiencing at that time. He always wanted to play Superman and was very bossy with the other children.

A review of Peter's educational records revealed a steady deterioration in the quality of his work over the past year in addition to an inability to remain focused and concentrate. He makes odd grimaces, snorts, swears, and so on when doing an assignment, or he will often pound the desk for a period of time. Peter will jump out of his seat and run out of the room disappearing for a few minutes to a half hour. His journal stories contained content about "drag queens," genital mutilation, sexual or physical abuse, and frequently had magical or impossible endings.

The report from the school psychologist indicated average intellectual functioning and academic weaknesses in reading, math, and written language. On a behavior rating scale, responses on the parent form reflected a clinically significant level of threatening behavior, hyperactivity, and impulsivity. Internalizing problems were revealed including depression and anxiety. On the teacher rating scale, it was reported that Peter had rule-breaking behaviors and internalizing problems of anxiety and depression in the clinically significant range. On the self-report scale, Peter demonstrated a substantial degree of social stress.

Psychiatric Consultation: Peter presented himself as a handsome, nonexpressive, very ambivalent 15-7 who became quite defensive when asked about his problems. Indicating he is unable to say what his problems are, Peter goes on to suggest that until 2 weeks ago, he experienced periodic dissatisfaction with schoolwork, but for the past 2 weeks his schoolwork has improved substantially.

When asked about making faces and snorting, Peter looks puzzled and tells me if a person is upset, his facial expression might change. Acknowledging that he mimics classmates and teachers, Peter says he chooses characteristics and focuses on them. Regarding his fantasy expressions, Peter cannot remember his dreams and neither does he know what his Magic Wish would be nor what he would like to change in his life.

Peter presents a substantial degree of immaturity, characterized by a narcissistic orientation to the world, a primary pleasure focus, and an inability to defer gratification. He is overly preoccupied with his own wishes and wants. Peter's anger flairs quickly when he does not achieve the pleasure or satisfaction of the moment, becomes anxious about anticipated tasks believing he is likely to fail, and is easily threatened by stressful situations. Confusion occurs readily since Peter lacks the capacity for objective thinking and is unable to predict the outcome of events. He is therefore confused when situations and circumstances turn out badly.

Peter is unable to focus or concentrate well, but this does not emanate from an attention-deficit difficulty since there is no early educational history of inattentiveness nor any preschool history of impulsivity or hyperactivity. Rather, his trouble in focusing springs from a preoccupation with his own wish fulfillment fantasies within school as a means of overriding his fears of failure. Because Peter lacks a satisfactory boundary between himself and adults, he will either overidentify with them or test their authority if he believes he can do so without serious consequences.

Peter readily translates his emotions into various facial grimaces and snorting sounds, but those do not represent motor tics or Tourette's Disorder.

Diagnosis: Oppositional Defiant Disorder

Recommendations: Family-oriented psychotherapy for Peter and his parents is recommended. Such psychotherapy should focus on his immature qualities, his self-serving attitudes, and his lack of awareness about the interpersonal consequences of his behavior.

Within the context of the classroom, the following issues should be addressed:

◆ **Interpersonal Consequences of His Behavior:** At this point in time, Peter avoids facing the extent to which his behavior probably alienates his peers. Although he thinks himself humorous, it is probable that his peers, viewing him as immature and therefore a source of embarrassment, may reject him. Inasmuch as he rationalizes his own silly and younger childlike behavior since it gratifies his ego, Peter misses the fact that others may laugh at him but not with him. Therefore, when he acts up and is immature, it is important to identify other children's reactions to his behavior, which is likely to be more motivating than any disciplinary action.

◆ **Stifling Role-Playing:** In school, as well as at home, Peter should be discouraged from engaging in mimicking others' behavior. Not only does this identify him for scapegoating, but it reinforces his sense of himself as a young child rather than a near adult. Peter may need to be reminded, in a supportive manner, that it is inappropriate to mimic others. If reminded frequently, over time, he may accomplish the goal of improved self-control, which will also lead to a higher level of self-regard.

♦ **Parental Clarifications:** It is important for Peter's parents to point out to Peter that his role-playing is not humorous and is characteristic of young children rather than mid-adolescents. Further, should he steal from them or become disrespectful, they should engage in growth-promoting discipline which entails punishment accompanied by a clarification that he is being disciplined because his parents wish him to grow up more and not because they want to take control of him. Such discipline might consist of depriving Peter of some pleasures for a time-limited period.

AUTHORS' COMMENTS: Peter's behaviors meet some of the characteristics of Oppositional Defiant Disorder. He often deliberately annoys people (mimicking, role-playing), often defies or refuses to comply with rules and requests, and is easily angered and resentful. Because of the seriousness of Peter's fantasies, his progress should be followed closely.

ANXIETY
DISORDERS

GENERALIZED
ANXIETY DISORDER

The Overanxious Disorder of Childhood found in the *DSM-III-R* is now incorporated into the Generalized Anxiety Disorder in the *DSM-IV.* Both are manifested by excessive or unrealistic worry about life events. In younger children, anxiety tends to be more focused. For example, they may experience a persistent worry about a specific person perceived as overly critical or threatening. However, as children mature, anxiety becomes more diffuse, permeating their judgment about peers, social relationships, academics, world affairs, athletic competence, and so forth. Anxiety may also center around future events, risk of injury, group acceptance, and meeting deadlines and expectations from others. At times, the appropriateness of past behaviors also elicits excessive concern. Children with this disorder may have exaggerated worry about minor occurrences, such as routine visits to the doctor and simple decision-making regarding peers and family activities. They may complain that others are mean to them or are treating them unfairly. In general, the focus of their worry shifts from one context to another but is always present to some degree and interferes with daily functioning.

Children with Generalized Anxiety Disorder are often described as overly mature, perfectionistic, and self-conscious. Because of their excessive self-doubts, they tend to overwork a given task, lack satisfaction with the outcome, fail to complete tasks on time, and seek frequent reassurance and approval from teachers, coaches, parents, and others. These children tend to judge their own abilities very harshly and are highly critical of their performance.

Physical complaints associated with anxiety are often reported and may take the form of nausea, headaches, sweaty hands, dizziness, insomnia, or shortness of breath. There may be motor restlessness, nail biting, hair pulling, and other nervous habits. These children complain of feeling "very nervous and unable to relax" and convey a general impression of tenseness.

Table of Contents for Generalized Anxiety Disorder

☑ CHECKLIST

GENERALIZED ANXIETY DISORDER

KEY	+	Presence
	-	Absence
	*	Associated Feature

MAJOR SYMPTOMS:

*	Inattention
-	Impulsivity
*	Abnormal Activity Level
-	Aggressiveness
-	Violation of Rules
-	Isolation/Withdrawal/Avoidance
-	Inability to Form/Maintain Relationships
*	Disturbances of Affect/Mood
+	Anxiety
*	Depression
-	Delusions/Hallucinations
+	Somatic Complaints
-	Oddities of Behavior
-	Language Impairment
-	Impaired Cognition
+	Significant Distress/Impairment in Important Areas of Functioning

INTERVIEW FORM
GENERALIZED
ANXIETY DISORDER

1. Does the child state persistent anxiety or worry about future events such as examinations, possibility of injury, meeting expectations, or inclusion in a peer group?
   ☐ Yes ☐ No

2. Is the child overly concerned about his or her past behaviors?   ☐ Yes ☐ No

3. Is the child overly preoccupied about competence in academic, social, or athletic situations?   ☐ Yes ☐ No

4. Does the child show excessive need for reassurance because of persistent self-doubt?   ☐ Yes ☐ No

5. Does the child frequently complain of headaches, stomachaches, and other somatic concerns when there is no physical basis for such?   ☐ Yes ☐ No

6. Does the child seem easily embarrassed or self-conscious?
   ☐ Yes ☐ No

7. Does the child seem unusually tense and unable to relax?
   ☐ Yes ☐ No

8. Does the child experience any sleep disturbances?
   ☐ Yes ☐ No

9. Does the child exhibit perfectionistic tendencies?
   ☐ Yes ☐ No

10. Does the child tend to judge himself or herself harshly?
    ☐ Yes ☐ No

11. Does the child delay completing work or projects?
    ☐ Yes ☐ No

12. Does the child express frequent complaints about peers and/or adults and describe them as mean or overly critical?
    ☐ Yes ☐ No

CASE SUMMARY

GENERALIZED ANXIETY DISORDER

Michael, C.A. 7–4

Reason for Referral: Michael's parents requested an evaluation to determine if their son has any special learning problems and to see if his tendency to withdraw should be given special attention. His school history reveals frequent absences over the past year.

Background Information: Michael's parents are both college graduates. Michael is a fraternal twin who, according to his parents, always has been developmentally behind his brother. His twin seems able to do everything quite well, and Michael is in his "shadow" as a result. Both children are in 2nd grade, in the same classroom, as the school is small and there is no other 2nd grade.

There is no significant medical history, other than recurrent ear infections for which tubes were placed in Michael's eardrums 1 year earlier. Reports from school indicate frequent visits to the nurse's office because of complaints of headaches.

Psychiatric Consultation: On examination, Michael was shy and withdrawn and eye contact was poor. He appeared nervous and tense throughout the evaluation even when frequent feedback and reassurance were offered to him. Much erasing on paper-and-pencil tasks as well as overall dissatisfaction with his own production were noted. Nail biting and chewing the collar of his shirt were observed.

A psychological evaluation revealed superior intellectual functioning (Full Scale IQ 123). The Bender was 1½ years delayed. In educational testing, no major weaknesses were found other than in written performance.

Projective testing suggested a great deal of anxiety, tension, and self-criticism. Michael tended to internalize feelings and use fantasy and intellectualization rather than seek interaction with others. A strong tendency to use avoidance in stressful situations was noted, contributing to his high rate of absence from school. He was quite constricted in his emotional expression, using short phrases and speaking in a very soft tone.

Diagnosis: Generalized Anxiety Disorder

Recommendations: Michael would benefit from systematic feedback and short-term assignments in a classroom setting where he would receive support and nonjudgmental reinforcement for his efforts. Tasks that would enhance his self-image and social standing in the classroom should be considered. Further exploration of his academic achievements and expectations should be pursued with Michael's parents, preferably through family counseling. Less emphasis on academics and more time spent in noncompetitive leisure activities, preferably away from his twin brother, would be of benefit.

AUTHORS' COMMENTS: Michael is experiencing anxiety and tension related to his performance and general competence. As a defense against anxiety, Michael self-criticizes, intellectualizes, and avoids stressful situations. Although of superior intelligence, he has become shy and withdrawn as a way of protecting himself from the judgments of others.

The fact that family counseling was recommended suggests that there may be pressures and expectations in the family that Michael feels unable to fulfill.

The clinical summary does not address Michael's social functioning. It is important to determine his ability to seek and maintain peer relationships. Also unknown is the extent of his worry when dealing with other daily situations; therefore, we do not know if his anxiety is primarily performance-oriented or pervades other aspects of his life.

CASE SUMMARY

GENERALIZED ANXIETY DISORDER AND DEPRESSIVE DISORDER NOT OTHERWISE SPECIFIED
Lucas, C.A. 14–3

Presenting Problem: Lucas is a 14-year-old, 8th grade adolescent male who was admitted to the hospital voluntarily by his father and the outpatient psychiatrist he had been seeing. Lucas apparently has become increasingly depressed, has voiced suicidal thoughts, and has been unable to function at school. He was on homebound tutoring, which he is now refusing. Lucas has extreme anxiety and difficulty going to school, which relates back to his earlier experiences of not being accepted and being made fun of by his peers. He states that when he was younger he was very obese and wore thick glasses making his eyes look very big. There was a time for about 2 years or so when he was accepted by his peers only because he was doing "bad things" (i.e., acting out, being offensive, and vandalizing). Lucas states now he knows that this is not right for him and hence, he is not accepted by his peers again. He also seems to have some major difficulties at home with his mother, who apparently has problems of her own, according to Lucas.

Lucas feels that his father doesn't like him and "he thinks he is better than me." Lucas' biggest fear always has been that he will not be able to fit in with the crowd. He was involved with the legal system one time when he used his BB gun at a bus stop. He had to go to Juvenile Court and states now that it was all straightened out. At age 12 or 13, Lucas used to go around on Halloween, squashing other people's pumpkins. Some impulsivity and mood lability is reported. However, these are not convincing enough to qualify for any major mood disorder.

Cognitively, Lucas is intact and no psychotic thinking is noted. He has drunk beer on a few occasions, last time being the day before yesterday. He has also experimented on a few occasions with marijuana. He has been treated with Prozac for almost a year, with no significant improvement.

Mental Status: Lucas presents himself as chubby but attractive, with adequate hygiene and grooming. His behavior during the interview was very cooperative. However, he did look anxious and nervous throughout the interview. Mild psychomotor agitation was noted. Speech was nonspontaneous but appropriate and goal directed. Affect was appropriate to his mood, which was slightly depressed and anxious. Lucas reported some difficulty falling asleep, and waking up in the middle of the night, but on the whole he sleeps about 9 hours or so a night. Appetite is "very good." There was no evidence of anhedonia, anergia, or pathological guilt. There were no somatic complaints nor difficulties with concentration. Suicidal ideation was presently denied. However, Lucas has had thoughts of wanting to hurt himself from time to time with no specific plans. There was no evidence of homicidal ideation, physical violence, assaultiveness, explosiveness, or out-of-control behavior. Thought processes and content show no thought disorder or looseness of association. There were no manic or hypomanic symptoms, nor hallucinations or delusional thinking. Motor tension and anxiety symptoms were present, without reaching panic-like levels. No evidence of phobic or obsessional thinking was noted. Lucas' intellectual functioning appeared to be average.

Diagnosis: This 14-year-old 8th grader has been having difficulties mainly in school, to the point that he has not been able to function in mainstream education. He has also had difficulties with homebound tutoring. Lucas' main difficulty started as a child when he was made fun of because of his obesity, as well as his extreme vision problems, which caused him to wear thick glasses. He feels that he is never accepted by his peers. He tried to do something to get in with the crowd, by vandalizing and other out-of-control behaviors. However, when he stopped doing that, Lucas again felt unable to make connections with his peers.

Lucas' main difficulties appear to be depression, as well as extreme anxiety which is related to peer difficulties and school problems. His presenting symptoms warrant a diagnosis of Generalized Anxiety Disorder and of Depressive Disorder Not Otherwise Specified. Treatment includes pharmacological intervention and hospitalization to stabilize mood and behavior.

AUTHORS' COMMENTS: Depressive symptoms can be part of an Anxiety Disorder. Lucas' failure to establish and maintain social relationships and be successful in school have caused him a great deal of distress, apprehension, and sadness. This report is a good example of a systematic approach to the multiple factors which need to be taken into account when considering a diagnosis.

SOCIAL PHOBIA
(SOCIAL ANXIETY DISORDER)

The *DSM-IV* has clarified some of the criteria pertaining to Social Phobia, specifically as it relates to children. As in the *DSM-III-R,* Social Phobia is defined as an ongoing fear when in the presence of unfamiliar people, or in any situation where judgment by others may occur. The *DSM-IV* notes that children with this disorder experience intense anxiety in anticipation of, or when exposed to, the situations they fear. In younger children, anxiety may be manifested by such behaviors as crying, tantrums, or avoiding social situations, because of their inability to identify the source of distress. They tend to be nonparticipants in group activities and prefer to remain on the sidelines. Older children are more aware of the unreasonable nature of their anxiety and as a result may become more anxious because of concerns that others may notice their distress. Physiological symptoms such as palpitations, shaky hands, diarrhea, sweating, stomachaches, and confusion often accompany this disorder. Many adolescents with Social Phobia were viewed as shy and inhibited in their early years. However, for others, the onset may be sudden, following an embarrassing or stressful experience. If the fears are present in most all social situations, the specifier of *Generalized* is given.

In spite of the child's capacity for age-appropriate social skills, the anxiety associated with this disorder is severe enough to impair social functioning and performance, not only in interactions with adults, but also in peer settings. Children with this disorder appear oversensitive to criticism, make harsh judgments about their own performance, show signs of low self-esteem, and lack assertiveness. They tend to avoid eye contact, are reluctant to volunteer answers in class, and may be hesitant and dysfluent when required to speak in front of a group. One of the most prevalent examples of Social Phobia involves the fear of speaking in public because of the potential embarrassment of being seen as foolish, inappropriate, or inadequate.

Occupational as well as academic pursuits may be significantly affected. For example, in school, these children experience intense test anxiety, worrying weeks ahead of time. In fact, they tend to perform poorly because of the emotional interference on their cognitive functioning. In general these children may present themselves as underachievers, but in actuality, the underlying anxiety of being judged is interfering with their ability to reach expected levels of performance.

Table of Contents for Social Phobia

☑ CHECKLIST
SOCIAL PHOBIA

KEY	
+	**Presence**
-	**Absence**
*	**Associated Feature**

MAJOR SYMPTOMS:

-	**Inattention**
-	**Impulsivity**
-	**Abnormal Activity Level**
-	**Aggressiveness**
-	**Violation of Rules**
+	**Isolation/Withdrawal/Avoidance**
*	**Inability to Form/Maintain Relationships**
-	**Disturbances of Affect/Mood**
+	**Anxiety**
*	**Depression**
-	**Delusions/Hallucinations**
+	**Somatic Complaints**
-	**Oddities of Behavior**
-	**Language Impairment**
-	**Impaired Cognition**
+	**Significant Distress/Impairment in Important Areas of Functioning**

INTERVIEW FORM
SOCIAL PHOBIA

1.   Has the person expressed fear about his or her perform-
     ance in social situations?   ☐ Yes ☐ No
     Describe the situation(s) where this occurs.

2.   Has the person specifically avoided anxiety-provoking situ-
     ations where he or she may be judged?   ☐ Yes ☐ No

3.   What are the reactions of the individual to anxiety-provoking
     social/performance circumstances? Describe.

4.   Is the person aware that his or her fears are excessive and
     unreasonable given the circumstances?   ☐ Yes ☐ No

5.   To what degree does anxiety interfere with social, school,
     or occupational functioning? Describe.

6.   Has there been a history of shy behavior and social
     inhibition?   ☐ Yes ☐ No

CASE SUMMARY

SOCIAL PHOBIA
Jill, C.A. 15–0

Presenting Problem: Jill came to the school psychologist seeking help because of increasingly severe panic attacks when entering the school building. She stated that she has tried to reduce her anxiety by taking tranquilizers in the morning before school and is considering not completing this semester.

Jill related that upon entering the school building she feels short of breath, begins to perspire, and has the urge to turn around and leave the grounds. Her daily schedule involves a speech and communication class during first period, where Jill is required to speak in public. She finds this increasingly threatening and anxiety provoking. She stated that she cannot speak as well as others and is afraid that class members will laugh at her attempts. Jill's fear has generalized to other classes when she is asked to participate verbally. Although her grades have dropped because of lack of oral participation, Jill has been unable to approach her teachers to explain her difficulties.

By contrast, Jill feels comfortable talking informally with friends. She has tried practicing her speeches with them and at home with her family, where she does well. It is only when she has to perform for others that panic strikes. A psychiatric consultation was recommended.

Diagnosis: Social Phobia

AUTHORS' COMMENTS: Jill's complaints meet the criteria for Social Phobia. When required to perform publicly, she experiences panic and anxiety attacks. Her fears of embarrassment are specific to a given situation as she is able to function normally at most other times. Jill has been unable to convey her difficulties to teachers. Her attempts to remedy the situation by self-medicating may place her at some risk for future substance abuse. Her self-referral to the school psychologist would suggest good insight and indicate a positive prognosis through therapy.

SEPARATION
ANXIETY DISORDER

There are no major changes in this disorder from the *DSM-III-R* to the *DSM-IV.* Children with Separation Anxiety Disorder manifest significant levels of anxiety which are specific to the separation from important others or from a familiar environment, such as home. The intensity of the anxiety experienced by the child is beyond what is expected for his or her developmental age. At times, the high degree of distress may resemble a panic attack.

When separated from important others, children with this disorder experience intense fears about the well-being of parents or of themselves; they often fantasize about possible accidents, serious illness, or traumatic events that may happen to them or to significant others to whom they feel attached. The identification of such fears usually gains in specificity as the child becomes older and more cognitively mature. Kindergarten-aged children are less likely to verbalize their specific fears when interviewed. Rather, they tend to show their distress in more nonverbal ways such as crying, screaming, kicking, or running away. In general, when separation occurs, children with this disorder will exhibit the full range of behaviors from social withdrawal, apathy, lack of involvement in play or work activities, to anger and physically aggressive behaviors towards those forcing separation. In addition, physical complaints are common, such as nausea, headaches, and vomiting.

Children experiencing Separation Anxiety Disorder usually have sleep disturbances and frequent nightmares. They may seek out their parents for comfort by requesting to sleep with them or appearing at the bedroom door during the night. The content of their nightmares is usually indicative of their specific fears concerning the safety of the family. Common themes in nightmares include attacks by monsters, fire, burglars, kidnappers, or the like. As a result of these fears, many children refuse to sleep at a friend's home or attend overnight camp. If they do leave the familiar environment, they are likely to be very unhappy, frequently requesting to call or return home.

At home these children may exhibit clinging behaviors inappropriate to their age, such as following a parent around the house. They tend to behave in a demanding manner, seeking constant attention, and placing undue stress on the family system. They may also show unusual eagerness to please, conformity, and task-oriented behavior when not threatened with separation. In general, this disorder seems to be more prevalent in children from close-knit, caring home environments. In many cases, the onset of this disorder follows a traumatic event in the child's life, such as school change, the loss of a pet or a family member, illness in the child or relative, or a move to new surroundings.

Although school refusal is frequently found in Separation Anxiety Disorder, the anxiety usually occurs in a variety of situations in which the separation from important others is the key factor. By contrast, what is commonly known as "school phobia" involves specific fears of school, regardless of the presence or absence of a significant attachment figure.

☑ CHECKLIST

SEPARATION ANXIETY DISORDER

KEY	**+** Presence
	- Absence
	* Associated Feature

MAJOR SYMPTOMS:

-	Inattention
-	Impulsivity
-	Abnormal Activity Level
*	Aggressiveness
-	Violation of Rules
+	Isolation/Withdrawal/Avoidance
*	Inability to Form/Maintain Relationships
*	Disturbances of Affect/Mood
+	Anxiety
*	Depression
-	Delusions/Hallucinations
+	Somatic Complaints
-	Oddities of Behavior
-	Language Impairment
-	Impaired Cognition
+	Significant Distress/Impairment in Important Areas of Functioning

INTERVIEW FORM
SEPARATION ANXIETY DISORDER

1. Does the child display temper tantrums, excessive crying, or panic reactions when about to be separated from parents or significant others? ☐ Yes ☐ No

2. When away from the major attachment figure, does the child behave in a socially withdrawn, apathetic, forlorn manner? ☐ Yes ☐ No

3. Does the child express unrealistic worry that something bad may happen to his or her family? ☐ Yes ☐ No

4. Does the child show clinging, shadowing behaviors towards important figure(s)? ☐ Yes ☐ No

5. Does the child complain of nausea, headaches, or vomiting when away from or anticipating separation from important others? ☐ Yes ☐ No

6. Does the child express unrealistic worry about animals or monsters, being lost, kidnapped, killed, or being a victim of an accident? ☐ Yes ☐ No

7. Does the child have nightmares with recurrent themes of being left alone? ☐ Yes ☐ No

8. Does the child refuse or is the child reluctant to sleep alone or away from home? ☐ Yes ☐ No

9. Does the child show a persistent pattern of school refusal in order to stay at home with attachment figure(s)?
    ☐ Yes ☐ No

10. Has there been a recent traumatic event in the child's life, such as death, accident, serious illness, or a recent move to new surroundings? ☐ Yes ☐ No Describe.

CASE SUMMARY

SEPARATION ANXIETY DISORDER
Bobby, C.A. 6–5

Reason for Referral: A psychiatric consultation was requested by the school because of ongoing concerns about Bobby's lack of adjustment to kindergarten and increasingly frequent absences from school. Background information is scant but indicates that he was enrolled in a preschool program 2 years ago for a short period of time and was withdrawn by mother because of significant behavioral difficulties. Last year mother registered Bobby for kindergarten, but he never attended due to considerable distress when required to go to school.

Mother again registered Bobby for kindergarten this year. He starts the morning at home by crying, screaming, and kicking. When mother tries to assist him in getting ready for school, he becomes physically aggressive with her. He also says he cannot go to school because of pains in his stomach and aches in his head.

Mother describes Bobby as a very clingy, demanding, and fearful child. At home, he follows her from room to room, won't allow her to talk on the phone, and becomes visibly distressed when she goes to the basement to do the laundry. Visits to the pediatrician were described as a "nightmare"; Bobby cries, won't let mother leave his side, and refuses to allow the doctor to interact or touch him. Mother reported that Bobby's behavioral difficulties started when he was 3 years old after a 1-week stay in the hospital for pneumonia. Since then, he experiences frequent nightmares and he fears that he will become sick again or that his mother will become seriously ill and leave him.

The school has attempted several strategies. Mother has been invited to attend school with Bobby, sit in the classroom, and drive him to and from school, rather than have him take the school bus. He has also been assigned a buddy to help him feel comfortable in the classroom. Despite several weeks of intervention, Bobby continues to manifest serious and significant distress about attending school and leaving his mother. This occurs whether he is at home, on the playground, at the doctor's office, or at his cousin's house.

Psychiatric Consultation: During the psychiatric interview, Bobby sat in his mother's lap facing away from the consultant, kept his thumb in his mouth, and showed no interest in the toys placed around the office. Mother described herself as a housewife with two older children, who reportedly have no behavior or school problems.

Diagnostic Impressions: Bobby presents many of the behaviors and characteristics associated with Separation Anxiety Disorder. It is recommended that a trial of medication be instituted to help reduce Bobby's level of anxiety so that the strategies offered by the school can have an opportunity to have a positive effect. Family-based therapy is also recommended in order to help Bobby gain independence from his mother and to assist her in management techniques conducive to a successful separation.

AUTHORS' COMMENTS: Bobby displays many of the behaviors found in children with Separation Anxiety Disorder. His hospitalization at age 3 may have triggered this persistent pattern of fears, unrealistic worries, nightmares, and clinging behaviors as well as aggressiveness when separation is forced.

POSTTRAUMATIC
STRESS DISORDER

There are no significant changes in Posttraumatic Stress Disorder from the *DSM-III-R* to the *DSM-IV.* Posttraumatic Stress Disorder is manifested by symptoms which begin to occur after exposure to a severe stressor. Stressors must be severe enough to be perceived as a serious threat to oneself or to others and may include such experiences as devastating natural disasters, war or violent confrontations, physical/sexual abuse, witnessing the death of a parent, or becoming aware of someone else's personal disaster. The person usually responds to such occurrences with intense fright, terror, or feelings of vulnerability. In younger children, this may be manifested by disruptive, unsettled, or agitated behavior.

One of the major characteristics of this disorder is the involuntary and unpredictable reexperiencing of the traumatic event. Individuals may recollect the episode in such a vivid manner that they behave as if it were happening again, expressing the same anxiety and severe distress that accompanied the event the first time. Children may not always be able to verbalize their perceptions, images, and thoughts associated with the stressor and may instead reenact it through play. The reexperiencing may also occur in the form of nightmares with frightening content. Anxiety can also surface when something in the environment symbolizes or is similar to the original traumatic event.

Another feature of Posttraumatic Stress Disorder is the need to avoid thinking about the event or avoid external situations which may remind the individual about the trauma. For example, statements such as "I don't want to talk about it," or "Don't remind me about it" are common. In addition, there may be a loss of memory for certain aspects of the traumatic experience. There are also marked feelings of detachment, emotional numbness, and withdrawal from people and activities once enjoyed. Associated features may include disturbances of sleep patterns, angry outbursts, intensified states of alertness, impulsivity, hopelessness, or loss of sustained concentration. In young children, physical complaints such as headaches and stomachaches are frequently reported. In older children, statements indicating inability or lack of desire to project into the future may be common, such as "I will never marry," "I will never drive a car," or "I'm going to die soon, anyway."

Onset of the symptoms of Posttraumatic Stress Disorder may occur immediately or several months after the traumatic event. Criteria for diagnosis are met when symptoms are present for more than 1 month.

Posttraumatic Stress Disorder differs from Adjustment Disorders in that in the latter, the stressor is not as severe and may be considered part of typical life experience(s). Stressors of a mild nature which are more likely to result in a diagnosis of Adjustment Disorders may include such events as change of school, divorce, or birth of another sibling. In Posttraumatic Stress Disorder the stressor is significantly more serious and threatening. Although people experience all degrees of stressors, it is the magnitude of the stressor and the individual's response to it that ultimately determines the presence of Posttraumatic Stress Disorder.

Table of Contents for
Posttraumatic Stress Disorder

☑ CHECKLIST

POSTTRAUMATIC
STRESS DISORDER

	+	**Presence**
KEY	-	**Absence**
	*	**Associated Feature**

MAJOR SYMPTOMS:

*	**Inattention**
*	**Impulsivity**
*	**Abnormal Activity Level**
*	**Aggressiveness**
-	**Violation of Rules**
+	**Isolation/Withdrawal/Avoidance**
*	**Inability to Form/Maintain Relationships**
+	**Disturbances of Affect/Mood**
+	**Anxiety**
*	**Depression**
*	**Delusions/Hallucinations**
*	**Somatic Complaints**
-	**Oddities of Behavior**
-	**Language Impairment**
-	**Impaired Cognition**
+	**Significant Distress/Impairment in Important Areas of Functioning**

INTERVIEW FORM

POSTTRAUMATIC
STRESS DISORDER

1. Has the child experienced a traumatic or threatening event?
    ☐ Yes ☐ No   Describe.

2. Does the child act as if he or she were reexperiencing the event by any of the following?

    ◆ Underlying distressing themes associated with the event through frequent verbal description or play
       ☐ Yes ☐ No

    ◆ Distressing dreams associated with the event
       ☐ Yes ☐ No

    ◆ Flashbacks, illusions, hallucinations, or actual behaviors that suggest that the child is reexperiencing the traumatic event   ☐ Yes ☐ No

    ◆ Significant distress in situations or circumstances that may symbolize or resemble the actual event
       ☐ Yes ☐ No

3. Is the child avoiding specific stimuli, or is there a generalized bluntness of affect in his or her responses as characterized by any of the following?

    ◆ Denial or avoidance of thoughts and feelings associated with the event   ☐ Yes ☐ No

    ◆ Avoidance of situations that may remind him or her of the event   ☐ Yes ☐ No

    ◆ Inability to remember parts of the traumatic event
       ☐ Yes ☐ No

    ◆ Decreased interest in previously enjoyed people and activities, or regression to earlier developmental states, such as soiling by young children
       ☐ Yes ☐ No

♦ Feelings of disconnectedness from others
    ☐ Yes ☐ No

♦ Diminished range of affective responses, such as the
   inability to give and/or receive affection
    ☐ Yes ☐ No

♦ Expressed unwillingness to plan for the future
    ☐ Yes ☐ No

4. Have any of the following arousal symptoms occurred after
   the traumatic event?

♦ Sleep disturbances   ☐ Yes ☐ No

♦ Irritability or angry outbursts   ☐ Yes ☐ No

♦ Decreased ability to concentrate   ☐ Yes ☐ No

♦ Intensified state of alertness   ☐ Yes ☐ No

♦ Easily alarmed   ☐ Yes ☐ No

♦ Physiological responses when placed in a situation
   similar to or symbolizing an aspect of the event,
   such as perspiring or shortness of breath
    ☐ Yes ☐ No

CASE SUMMARY

POSTTRAUMATIC STRESS DISORDER
Larry, C.A. 5–5

Reason for Referral: Larry's teacher was concerned about Larry's high energy level, short attention span, inability to sit still and complete work independently, need for constant reassurance, and aggressive behavior towards others. In particular, Larry displays excessive attention-seeking behaviors. Academically, he appears to be capable of doing the work but cannot accomplish anything if not given one-to-one attention.

Family and Social History: Larry is an only child. Mother reports a history of wife and child abuse by Larry's father. Father was the primary caretaker during infancy while the mother worked two jobs. The physical abuse incurred by Larry was primarily aimed at his legs, lower body, and backside. He was also reportedly tied to a chair with his mouth taped, and he was put in a closet alone for hours at a time.

Mother notes that Larry exhibits a quick temper, stubbornness, and aggressiveness towards others. At other times, Larry appears sullen for no particular reason. He also has many fears. At home he follows his mother around and needs constant reassurance.

Clinical Assessment: Larry's intellectual functioning is at least on the High Average range. There is a large discrepancy between cognitive and emotional functioning.

During the evaluation, Larry made little eye contact, kept his voice quite loud, and often attempted to leave his seat. Projective testing results had an extremely immature quality to them with signs of emotional lability, aggressive attitudes, and a high level of anxiety. There were themes of hostility, sadness, and fears of harm and rejection.

Psychiatric Consultation: Larry came to the interview willingly. He sat fairly still in his chair while he talked almost incessantly. He related in a very engaging, lively manner and was most open and cooperative.

Larry's vocabulary was precocious, as was his capacity for comprehension and concept formation. At the same time, the content of his speech was rambling and rather confused. He claimed that he occasionally hears voices, but it was difficult to determine the significance of this statement. He admitted that he occasionally feels sad but denied any suicidal feelings. He was able to describe some of the physical abuse that he experienced in the past at the hands of his father.

Larry is experiencing a Posttraumatic Stress Disorder, secondary to his having been physically abused in the past. He is also very disorganized and erratic. The combination of these problems constitutes a serious emotional disturbance. Consideration should be made for a special classroom placement for children with emotional disorders. Larry's chance to recover from his present emotional difficulties strongly depends upon family therapy.

AUTHORS' COMMENTS: Larry's history of abuse constitutes a severe traumatic event. Although this occurred several years ago, he still manifests many of the symptoms associated with this trauma: anxiety, angry outbursts, depression, impulsivity, and inability to maintain concentration. Hallucinations may be present. Larry's unconscious recollection of being forced to remain in a chair with his mouth taped may manifest itself by his inability to sit still and his incessant talking while seated.

Other areas that could have been productively explored include Larry's sleep patterns and social interactions outside of school. The report noted that Larry experiences significant fears but did not address their content. However, considering the major stressor and Larry's subsequent behaviors, the diagnosis of Posttraumatic Stress Disorder appears appropriate.

OBSESSIVE-COMPULSIVE DISORDER

There are minor differences between the *DSM-III-R* and *DSM-IV* with respect to Obsessive-Compulsive Disorder. The *DSM-IV* has added two exclusionary statements in order to meet criteria. The diagnosis of Obsessive-Compulsive Disorder is *not* made if the obsessive or compulsive behaviors, activities, or thoughts are restricted to a specific disorder; for example, excessive eating in Eating Disorders, preoccupation with drugs in Substance Use Disorders. The second exclusionary statement refers to the need to rule out physiological causes as the trigger of obsessions and/or compulsions before a diagnosis of Obsessive-Compulsive Disorder is given. In addition, the *DSM-IV* has added a specifier: ***With Poor Insight.*** This relates to the individual's inability to recognize the unreasonable nature of the thoughts, ideas, images, and behaviors. This specifier does not necessarily apply to young children because their level of cognitive development may limit this type of insight.

Obsessive-Compulsive Disorder consists of recurrent obsessions or compulsions of sufficient severity as to consume inordinate amounts of the individual's time, cause significant distress, and result in impairment of overall or daily functioning. Obsessions are defined as intrusive, inappropriate, and persistent ideas, thoughts, impulses, or images which the individual attempts to suppress, ignore, or replace with other thoughts or behaviors. They are unlikely to be based on worry about real life events. Obsessions are experienced as being alien, unprovoked, and out of the individual's control. However, there is awareness that they are generated from within the person's mind. This recognition may not be present in young children. When attention is drawn to the child's inappropriate or excessive behavior, he or she may state, "I don't know what's making me do this."

Compulsions are defined as repetitive actions performed by the individual in order to alleviate the distress caused by obsessions. They are excessive activities or mental acts which may not be related to the thoughts or behaviors the individual is trying to suppress. Children may be aware that their behaviors are abnormal or inappropriate and may be afraid of "going crazy." They may attempt to be secretive, displaying more of the obsessive-compulsive behaviors at home when away from peers and direct adult supervision. Symptoms tend to increase during times of stress.

In general, children do not seek intervention themselves for obsessive-compulsive behavior; instead, a referral for treatment is more often made by an adult who knows the child. Teachers are more likely to refer because of poor schoolwork, difficulty concentrating, and rigid or perfectionistic tendencies.

☑ CHECKLIST

OBSESSIVE-COMPULSIVE DISORDER

KEY	+	Presence
	-	Absence
	*	Associated Feature

MAJOR SYMPTOMS:

-	Inattention
+	Impulsivity
-	Abnormal Activity Level
-	Aggressiveness
-	Violation of Rules
*	Isolation/Withdrawal/Avoidance
-	Inability to Form/Maintain Relationships
*	Disturbances of Affect/Mood
+	Anxiety
*	Depression
-	Delusions/Hallucinations
-	Somatic Complaints
+	Oddities of Behavior
-	Language Impairment
-	Impaired Cognition
+	Significant Distress/Impairment in Important Areas of Functioning

INTERVIEW FORM
OBSESSIVE-COMPULSIVE DISORDER

1. Does the child manifest recurrent and inappropriate ideas, thoughts, impulses, or images? ☐ Yes ☐ No Describe.

2. Does the child engage in frequent and repetitive acts, such as "constantly" checking to see if the lights are off, erasing the same written product, or going back and forth to sharpen a pencil without need? ☐ Yes ☐ No   Describe.

3. Does the child have difficulty staying on task?
    ☐ Yes ☐ No

4. Has the child been described as rigid, perfectionistic, or unbending? ☐ Yes ☐ No

5. To what degree have these behaviors interfered with the child's daily functioning? Describe.

CASE SUMMARY
OBSESSIVE-COMPULSIVE DISORDER
Steven, C.A. 15–4

Reason for Referral: Steven was brought to the attention of the school psychologist because of continued disciplinary problems.   He has a long-term pattern of tardiness to school, roaming the halls, leaving school grounds without permission, and unexcused absences.   In-school suspensions and detentions have not modified his behavior.

Relevant History: Steven lives with his mother, who works two jobs.   Father left the family when Steven was 2 years of age, with no further contact.   Steven is an only child and reportedly is responsible for all his daily living needs.

Clinical Interview: Steven presented himself as a well-groomed adolescent of average height and weight for his age. He was articulate and appeared to be of at least average intelligence.   Upon inquiry about his disciplinary problems, Steven revealed that his school problems may be related to his overpreoccupation with his dog "Sammy."   Before leaving the house every morning, Steven checks the dog's pen to be sure there is adequate food and water and the lock is secure. He states that as soon as he gets to the front door, he starts questioning and turns around, goes to the backyard, and repeats the same routine again.   These behaviors occur several times every morning so that Steven misses his school bus and either walks to school or stays home.   On occasion, Steven has even left school in the middle of the day to check on Sammy.   He acknowledges that he is violating school rules but states that he can't help himself.

His tardiness to class and roaming the halls appear related to a need to check whether he has all of his belongings.   Steven stated that before he leaves any class, he clears his desk and places all his materials in his backpack; however, upon leaving the classroom and walking down the hall he starts questioning whether he left some item in the room and has to return immediately. Consequently, he is late for his next class, interrupts the class already in session, and is invariably caught without a pass by the hall monitor. Steven stated that he knows his worries are "weird," but he cannot put the thoughts out of his mind.

When asked if he experiences such thoughts and behaviors at other times, Steven stated that he is usually in trouble with his mother at home because of compliance issues. Because of her work schedule, she makes requests from Steven to run errands, which he never gets around to doing because he finds it impossible to leave the house without checking and rechecking his dog's condition and whether he has his money, the list, the key, and the locks. He stated that he cannot walk half a block down the street without returning to check something.

Psychiatric Consultation: A psychiatric consultation was sought for Steven, and the diagnosis of Obsessive-Compulsive Disorder was made. Recommendations included pharmacological intervention as well as family counseling and behavioral modification strategies.

AUTHORS' COMMENTS: Steven presents the typical symptomatology associated with Obsessive-Compulsive Disorder. He reports obsessive thoughts, knows that they are irrational, but cannot control them, nor can he cease to perform the compulsive actions associated with his thoughts. Steven's pathology has been misinterpreted by the school and his mother as intentional violation of rules and noncompliant behavior. With a combination of medication, therapy, and education about the characteristics of this disorder to mother and school officials, Steven would be less likely to suffer disciplinary consequences.

SELECTIVE MUTISM

Besides the change of the name to Selective Mutism in the *DSM-IV* from Elective Mutism in the *DSM-III-R,* changes in criteria include specified duration of this condition for at least 1 month, excluding the first month of school, and exemption of immigrants who may not be fluent in the host language.

Selective Mutism is characterized by a persistent refusal to speak in social situations, such as school or with peers, despite the ability and willingness to speak in other situations. Impairment in social and school functioning is likely to occur because of reluctance to communicate with others. Children with this disorder may attempt communication by nonverbal gesturing or monosyllabic utterances. It is not uncommon for such children to point to what they want, to shake or nod their heads when asked a question, or to relate their needs through whispers. They are often described as very shy, clinging, and socially withdrawn in unfamiliar situations. They may suffer from emotional badgering and teasing by their peers partly because of their limited verbal output. School refusal may be associated with this disorder. However, in the home, these children may be quite talkative, oppositional, demanding, and prone to temper tantrums.

Some of these children may present articulation and/or language delays. Anxiety Disorders, like Social Phobia, as well as significant psychosocial stressors such as hospitalization, and/or a new school environment, may also be associated with Selective Mutism.

Table of Contents for Selective Mutism

☑ CHECKLIST
SELECTIVE MUTISM

KEY	+	Presence
	-	Absence
	*	Associated Feature

MAJOR SYMPTOMS:

-	Inattention
-	Impulsivity
-	Abnormal Activity Level
*	Aggressiveness
-	Violation of Rules
+	Isolation/Withdrawal/Avoidance
*	Inability to Form/Maintain Relationships
-	Disturbances of Affect/Mood
*	Anxiety
*	Depression
-	Delusions/Hallucinations
-	Somatic Complaints
+	Oddities of Behavior
*	Language Impairment
-	Impaired Cognition
*	Significant Distress/Impairment in Important Areas of Functioning

INTERVIEW FORM

SELECTIVE MUTISM

1. Does the child have the ability to speak and comprehend language? ☐ Yes ☐ No   If yes,

2. Does the child persistently refuse to speak in most social situations, including school? ☐ Yes ☐ No

3. How does the child communicate? Describe.

4. Does the child exhibit any of the following behaviors?

   ♦ Excessive shyness   ☐ Yes ☐ No

   ♦ Clinging   ☐ Yes ☐ No

   ♦ Social withdrawal   ☐ Yes ☐ No

   ♦ School refusal   ☐ Yes ☐ No

   ♦ Oppositional behavior   ☐ Yes ☐ No

5. Has the child been diagnosed as having a speech disorder? ☐ Yes ☐ No

6. Has the child been exposed to a physical or emotional trauma? ☐ Yes ☐ No   Explain.

7. For how long has the child refused to speak in social situations? Describe.

8. Has the refusal to speak continued beyond the first month of school? ☐ Yes ☐ No

9. Has the child recently relocated to a region where another language is spoken? ☐ Yes ☐ No

CASE SUMMARY

SELECTIVE MUTISM
Thomas, C.A. 7–3

Clinical Summary: Thomas was referred for a complete evaluation because of his refusal to speak at school. This problem became apparent when he started nursery school at age 3. He would not speak to other students or teachers and spent his school days sitting apart and watching. At home he spoke with his family and would speak to other children outside of school. With a lot of encouragement, he had started to speak in a whisper to his teacher and to speak to other children on the playground. However, other children tended to ignore him, and he seemed "odder" as he got older. One year ago he was referred to a psychiatric clinic and a behavior management program was begun to facilitate eye contact and interaction. Because of lack of progress, the current evaluation was requested.

There was no significant medical history other than several ear infections. He had tubes inserted twice but currently has normal hearing. The parents felt that his receptive and expressive language skills were normal. They felt that he was not affectionate and was possibly depressed. The family consisted of mother and father, both high school graduates, Thomas, and a 5-year-old sibling, who had also been very quiet upon entering school.

On examination, the boy made little eye contact, keeping a baseball cap pulled down over his forehead at all times. He responded to instructions but said nothing. During evaluation sessions, Thomas' mother requested that she be allowed to sit outside the examiner's room. Thomas performed above the 2nd grade level in all academic tasks but would not verbalize. A speech and language evaluation was accomplished by the mother administering the test items. His receptive and expressive language skills were normal.

Intellectual assessment indicated average results. Personality assessment suggested an array of ego deficits, including strong dependency needs, strong feelings of insecurity, and lack of trust. Control over his own verbalizations was felt to represent his attempt to exert control over his life in one of the few ways he could. All evaluators agreed on a diagnosis of Selective Mutism. Recommendations were made for a psychiatrically based day-treatment program.

AUTHORS' COMMENTS: Although Thomas understands language and can speak, he has persistently refused to do so in school. He has exhibited such behaviors for the past 4 years. From the descriptions of his symptoms, he presents himself as an overly dependent youngster who will only perform the required tasks in his mother's presence. As stated by the psychiatrist, Thomas' refusal to speak suggests an attempt to exert control over some aspect of his life.

Thomas demonstrated some of the additional features associated with this disorder. He was uncooperative during the examination, refusing to follow many of the doctor's requests. Social withdrawal and inability to initiate peer interaction were also noted. These behaviors meet the diagnostic criteria for Selective Mutism. The recommendation for such a restrictive treatment illustrates the extent and severity of his disorder.

MOOD
DISORDERS

MOOD DISORDERS

The Mood Disorders section of this book includes Major Depressive Disorder, Bipolar I Disorder, Bipolar II Disorder, Dysthymic Disorder, and Cyclothymic Disorder. In order to reach a diagnosis for any of these disorders, it is necessary to explore history, presence, and severity of single mood episodes: *Depressive, Manic, Hypomanic,* and *Mixed.* The episodes alone do not constitute a diagnostic category, but their symptoms are crucial in describing and differentiating a given mood disorder. Symptoms for each episode fall into two broad categories: Depressive and Manic.

The next section describes the individual episodes, followed by a comprehensive Interview Form of Depressive and Manic symptoms. A Summary Chart has been provided to better illustrate the organization of mood disorders according to type of mood symptoms, their severity, and prior history. Following the Summary Chart is a brief narrative of each mood disorder and several Case Summaries.

EPISODES

Major Depressive Episode

A Major Depressive Episode is primarily characterized by a significant loss of interest or pleasure in previously enjoyed activities and by a pervasively depressed mood, lasting at least 2 weeks. In children and adolescents, the episode may be manifested by irritability rather than sadness. In all cases, a Major Depressive Episode involves a cluster of symptoms affecting all areas of the individual's functioning. The presence of depressed mood in children is usually inferred from the observations of others who know them, such as parents and teachers, but should also be explored through a clinical interview with the child to uncover feelings that may not be readily observable by others.

In the affective area, there may be feelings of guilt, sadness, crying spells, self-reproach, a sense of worthlessness, feelings of inadequacy, and harsh judgments of self. Children may state that they are "dumb," "stupid," "worthless," "useless," "ugly," or "guilty." When asked about the future, children who are depressed tend to report a sense of hopelessness and pessimism. Other symptoms may include anxiety, preoccupation with physical health, fears, and panic attacks. Suicidal ideation or thoughts of death may be present. In very young children, depression may be manifested by irritability and anger, lack of cooperation with adult requests, and apathy towards their environment.

In the cognitive area, there may be negative thinking about self and others as well as difficulties in recall, concentration, and decision-making. Decreased motivation is further affected by fatigue, apathy, or slowness of response. There is marked loss of interest in hobbies, school, friends, sports, and other activities previously enjoyed. In the social/behavioral domain, acting-out tendencies or decreased interaction with others are present. These children may misinterpret events and assign blame to themselves when the events are clearly out of their control.

Depression may be manifested by negativistic behaviors, angry outbursts, blaming others, and low frustration tolerance. Especially in adolescents, there is increased sensitivity to being criticized or rejected by others. There also may be poor hygiene, substance abuse, and increased lack of cooperation at home and in school.

Psychomotor disturbances may be present. They could take the form of increased agitation such as inability to sit still, or decreased levels of energy such as slowed body movements, poverty of speech, and complaints of fatigue. In the vegetative domain, depressed children may also show disturbances of sleep patterns such as sleeping too much or not enough. Appetite changes may be noted by either weight loss or gain.

☑ CHECKLIST

MAJOR DEPRESSIVE EPISODE

KEY	+	Presence
	-	Absence
	*	Associated Feature

MAJOR SYMPTOMS:

*	Inattention
-	Impulsivity
+	Abnormal Activity Level
-	Aggressiveness
-	Violation of Rules
+	Isolation/Withdrawal/Avoidance
*	Inability to Form/Maintain Relationships
+	Disturbances of Affect/Mood
*	Anxiety
+	Depression
*	Delusions/Hallucinations
+	Somatic Complaints
-	Oddities of Behavior
-	Language Impairment
-	Impaired Cognition
+	Significant Distress/Impairment in Important Areas of Functioning

Manic Episode

A Manic Episode is primarily defined by an elevated or irritable mood, which has a distinct, recognizable onset and lasts at least 1 week. The elevated mood is characterized by euphoria and expansiveness. For example, the individual may appear excessively happy or high and engage in numerous and random interactions with others. There may also be pleasure-seeking and risk-taking activities such as buying sprees, promiscuous sexual activity, and high-speed driving.

The irritable mood may be more predominant in some individuals, particularly when obstacles are placed in the way of their wants and desires. An individual with Manic Episode may fluctuate between elevated and irritable moods. In general, Manic Episodes are most common in adults but can occur in adolescents.

Several other characteristics are present in a Manic Episode. There is grandiosity and inflated self-esteem, manifested by statements of knowing everything or claiming to be able to do anything competently or better than anyone else. People experiencing a Manic Episode may sleep significantly less than they normally do, with no complaints of feeling tired or fatigued. Changes in speech pattern and content may also be evident during the episode. Individuals may talk constantly, going from one topic to another, sometimes accompanied by flamboyant gesturing. In contrast, the speech of people with an irritable mood takes on a belligerent content and tone.

In children, manic behavior is characterized by euphoria, excessive and inappropriate cheerfulness, giddiness, and silly behavior. Speech is rushed and verbose, with grandiose and/or delusional content and flights of ideas.

During the Manic Episode, individuals may have difficulty focusing and concentrating and have trouble selecting relevant from irrelevant stimuli. They may get distracted by noises, details, or objects in their environment. Distractibility, impulsivity, overactivity, and poor judgment are also found in individuals with Attention-Deficit/Hyperactivity Disorder. However, the Attention-Deficit/Hyperactivity Disorder syndrome becomes apparent at an earlier age, has a chronic course, and lacks the significantly elevated mood common to the Manic Episode.

☑ CHECKLIST

MANIC EPISODE

KEY	**+**	**Presence**
	-	**Absence**
	*	**Associated Feature**

MAJOR SYMPTOMS:

*	**Inattention**
+	**Impulsivity**
+	**Abnormal Activity Level**
-	**Aggressiveness**
-	**Violation of Rules**
-	**Isolation/Withdrawal/Avoidance**
-	**Inability to Form/Maintain Relationships**
+	**Disturbances of Affect/Mood**
-	**Anxiety**
-	**Depression**
*	**Delusions/Hallucinations**
-	**Somatic Complaints**
-	**Oddities of Behavior**
-	**Language Impairment**
-	**Impaired Cognition**
+	**Significant Distress/Impairment in Important Areas of Functioning**

Hypomanic Episode

The Hypomanic Episode shares the same symptomatology as the Manic Episode described previously. The difference is one of severity in that the person's daily functioning is not as significantly impaired in the Hypomanic Episode as it is in the Manic Episode.

☑ CHECKLIST

HYPOMANIC EPISODE

KEY	+	Presence
	-	Absence
	*	Associated Feature

MAJOR SYMPTOMS:

*	Inattention
+	Impulsivity
+	Abnormal Activity Level
-	Aggressiveness
-	Violation of Rules
-	Isolation/Withdrawal/Avoidance
-	Inability to Form/Maintain Relationships
+	Disturbances of Affect/Mood
-	Anxiety
-	Depression
-	Delusions/Hallucinations
-	Somatic Complaints
-	Oddities of Behavior
-	Language Impairment
-	Impaired Cognition
-	Significant Distress/Impairment in Important Areas of Functioning

Mixed Episode

The Mixed Episode is characterized by the presence of both the Major Depressive Episode and Manic Episode within the same day, for nearly every day, over a period of at least 1 week. The symptoms present in the Mixed Episode are severe enough to interfere significantly with the individual's functioning and may require hospitalization.

GENERAL INTERVIEW FORM

MOOD DISORDERS
Depressive Symptoms

1. Has the child been unusually sad, unhappy, or tearful?
   ☐ Yes ☐ No

2. Is the child unresponsive or apathetic towards previously enjoyed activities?   ☐ Yes ☐ No

3. Has there been a change in the child's eating patterns?
   ☐ Yes ☐ No   Describe. Indicate any fluctuation in weight.

4. Does the child appear hopeless and helpless?
   ☐ Yes ☐ No

5. Does the child appear tired or complain of frequent fatigue?   ☐ Yes ☐ No

6. Are there signs of hypercritical judgments or guilt-ridden statements?   ☐ Yes ☐ No

7. Has the child become excessively fearful or avoidant of people or situations?   ☐ Yes ☐ No

8. Has the child become overly preoccupied with his or her physical health?   ☐ Yes ☐ No

9. Are there signs of recurrent suicidal thoughts or gestures?
   ☐ Yes ☐ No

10. Is the child described as withdrawn and isolated?
    ☐ Yes ☐ No

11. Have there been any changes in the child's personal hygiene habits?   ☐ Yes ☐ No

12. Has school performance declined to a marked degree?
    ☐ Yes ☐ No

Manic Symptoms

13. Has the child been in an unusually "high," giddy, euphoric, or expansive mood?   ☐ Yes ☐ No

14. Is the child engaging in excesses of behavior, such as talking too much or being indiscriminately friendly?
    ☐ Yes ☐ No

15. Does the child engage in excessive risk-taking and/or pleasure-seeking activities?   ☐ Yes ☐ No

16. Does the child state that he or she knows everything, is better than everyone else, and can do anything?
    ☐ Yes ☐ No

17. Has the child's speech been more rushed, rapid, and wordy?   ☐ Yes ☐ No

18. Does the child's content of speech suggest delusional thinking?   ☐ Yes ☐ No

19. Does the child seem physically "overactive"?
    ☐ Yes ☐ No

For Both Depressive/Manic Symptoms

20. Has the child shown irritability, grouchiness, and low frustration tolerance?   ☐ Yes ☐ No

21. Has there been a change in the child's sleep patterns?
    ☐ Yes ☐ No

22. Has the child become oppositional, aggressive, and increasingly uncooperative?   ☐ Yes ☐ No

23. Does the child show difficulties in concentration, attention to tasks, and decision-making skills?   ☐ Yes ☐ No

24. Is the child engaging in substance abuse?
    ☐ Yes ☐ No   Describe.

NOTE: The following chart organizes Mood Disorders according to the type of mood symptoms, their severity, and prior history.

Mood Disorders Summary Chart						
DISORDERS	**MOOD SYMPTOMS/EPISODES**					
	Depressive		**Manic**		**Mixed**	
	Current	Prior History	Current	Prior History	Current	Prior History
Major Depressive Disorder	E	{E}				
Bipolar I Disorder:						
Single Manic			E			
Hypomanic			S	{S}		{S}
Manic		{E}	E	{E}		{E}
Mixed		{E}		{E}	E	{E}
Depressed	E			{E}		{E}
Bipolar II Disorder	E	{E}	S	{S}		
Dysthymia	S					
Cyclothymia					S	

KEY

E   **Episode - Severe**
{E} **Episode may or may not have been present**
S   **Symptoms - Mild**
{S} **Symptoms may or may not have been present**

<u>DISORDERS</u>

Major Depressive Disorder

Major Depressive Disorder is defined by one or more Major Depressive Episodes without the presence of the manic features characteristic of a Manic Episode. In order for a Major Depressive Disorder to be diagnosed, the symptoms of depression must be present for most of the day, nearly every day, for at least 2 weeks. The symptoms of depression must be of significant severity as to be able to differentiate between the person's prior mood, behavior, and overall functioning and his or her present status. The Checklist for Major Depressive Episode (p. 103) applies to this disorder.

CASE SUMMARY
MAJOR DEPRESSIVE DISORDER
Carol, C.A. 15–3

Presenting Problem: This is the first hospitalization for Carol, a 10th grader, as a result of an exacerbation of suicidal ideation, which has been ongoing for the past 2 months. She approached her mother and told her that she was exhausted and needed help. Apparently Carol has been having a great deal of trouble mobilizing herself to take care of her usual activities. She has been unable to attend school and has been absent 33 days to date. Carol claims that she cannot go to school because she is very self-conscious and feels that she does not "fit in." She noticed that she has been significantly depressed for the last 2 to 3 years. She has experienced difficulty falling asleep and ruminates through the night. She then oversleeps the next day when she should be in school. Carol reports that she feels very alienated from her peers. She has lost interest in her usual activities, which in the past have included cheerleading. She describes herself as shy and something of a loner. She knows that she has many obsessive traits and is a perfectionist. She is also very self-denigrating. Carol has been having increasing suicidal thoughts because she feels unable to fit in with her peers and to maintain appropriate behavior for her age. Carol also has a history of obsessive-compulsive symptoms with much ruminative worry and compulsions that send her on bathroom rituals. Carol appears quite anxious when pressed to discuss these rituals, but the mother indicated that they involve compulsively having to dry herself when on the toilet and inability to get off the toilet that sometimes lasts for 2 to 3 hours until her mother helps her to do so.

Carol has had some outpatient psychotherapy for about a year. For a while she was maintained on Prozac. However, this did not seem helpful, and when the dosage was raised she began to experience side effects including visual hallucinations.

Mental Status Examination: Carol presents herself as a casually dressed, 15-year-old female who appears her stated age.

She is quite guarded, subdued, and anxious in the interview and is clearly depressed, but she tries to be cooperative. Her psychomotor functioning shows retardation. Her speech is decreased and affect is blunted. Mood is depressed. She describes difficulty falling asleep, some middle of the night awakening, and sometimes an increased need for sleep. Her appetite has been decreased and she experiences anhedonia, anergia, guilt, and difficulty concentrating. Her libido is decreased. She describes ongoing suicidal ideation but no fixed plan. There is no homicidal ideation. Her thinking is logical and goal directed, but she appears somewhat rigid. There are no hallucinations nor delusions. There is no evidence of formal thought disorder although she has a mild paranoid coloration to her thinking. She describes no phobias. She does describe obsessions in the form of self-denigrating thoughts and obsessional worry. Her attention span is decreased; she can repeat seven digits forwards and six digits backwards. She can do serial seven calculations well. Her fund of knowledge is average. Immediate, recent, and remote memories are intact. She can abstract proverbs and her intellectual functioning appears to be in the high average range.

Diagnosis: This 15-year-old presents with a history of worsening depression with severe neurovegetative symptoms and obsessive-compulsive behaviors. The following diagnoses are given: Major Depressive Disorder, recurrent, severe, and Obsessive-Compulsive Disorder.

Recommendations: The patient requires hospitalization because of suicidal ideation and severe depression. Pharmacological interventions were determined.

AUTHORS' COMMENTS: Carol presents a long-term history of depression which is affecting all areas of functioning (eating, sleeping, social activities, and school attendance and performance). In addition, her self-punitive comments and suicidal ideation are severe enough to warrant immediate attention and hospitalization. She also displays obsessive-compulsive behaviors (bathroom rituals) which are disrupting her overall functioning, causing her more distress, and warranting an additional diagnosis of Obsessive-Compulsive Disorder. The case summary did not include background history or investigation of possible traumatic stressors in her life.

Bipolar Disorders

Bipolar Disorders have been divided into two major disorders: *Bipolar I* and *Bipolar II* Disorders. Bipolar I Disorders consist of one or more Manic Episodes. There may be periods of time between Manic Episodes in which the individual meets the criteria for either Major Depressive Episode, Hypomanic Episode, or Mixed Episode. Bipolar I Disorders are classified according to the most recent episode.

Bipolar II Disorders consist of one or more Major Depressive Episodes with at least one Hypomanic Episode. The presence of either a Manic Episode or Mixed Episode would warrant a classification of a Bipolar I Disorder rather than a Bipolar II Disorder.

CASE SUMMARY
BIPOLAR I DISORDER
Matt, C.A. 16–0

Presenting Problem: This is the first hospitalization for this 16-year-old male, who has the chief complaint of "mental breakdown with stressors that made me go inward and introspective." This young man has a history of Attention-Deficit/ Hyperactivity Disorder diagnosed last year. Matt has used alcohol once or twice and was smoking but has stopped use of both approximately 4 months ago. He was placed on medication and became increasingly depressed and isolative this past fall, with increasing peer difficulty and academic pressures. He was receiving therapy. This youngster states that he has an internal mental father "inside of me." He states that this "mental father" made him lose his "old personality," which he was not proud of, and take a new one which he likes. He states that "I stare at teachers and we create things in my mind." He states that he thought that the mental father had started being part of his life about 8 to 9 months ago. He talked about last week when he thought his mental father had "passed away" and he became violent, broke doors down in his house, and became assaultive. He now talks about seeing "astrobodies," which are the "center of everything," "a compound of desire and emotions." He also states that he sees auras around his body and around other people and sees five or six hands when he stares at his own hand. He states that he has gotten involved in occult interests and, through some of his father's books, he discovered Hatha Yoga. He states that occasionally he hears voices. His concentration has become increasingly impaired. He has not felt suicidal or homicidal but states that he was extremely depressed, was unmotivated, would not come out of his room, and would just read his occult books. He states his appetite was decreased and he was not sleeping the way he had been before.

Mental Status Examination: Matt is a well-developed, well-nourished adolescent male, appearing his stated age. He was well dressed and his hair was combed neatly. His speech was somewhat tangential and his affect mildly blunted. His mood was depressed. He states that at times he has been anhedonic and anergic but is feeling somewhat better now. He has great difficulty concentrating. This youngster has circumstantiality and tangentiality. He has had hallucinations in which he hears voices but does not know what they are saying. He states he sees auras around his body and his hands and has an elaborate delusional system which combines some of his occult readings and yoga philosophy with his own theories. He states that "I lost my old personality that I was not proud of because of my mental father." He states that this mental father is something inside of him that manipulates vehicles in the universe. Matt believes in ESP and thinks that there are astrobodies that are the center of everything and that they are compounds of desires and emotions. He denies paranoia but has some thought insertion, thought control, and thought broadcasting. He denies anxiety, phobias, or obsessions.

Cognitively, Matt is oriented in all three areas. Attention span is decreased as he was unable to do digit span. He did calculations quickly and well. Fund of knowledge is average. Immediate, recent, and remote memories are grossly intact. Insight and judgment are very poor. Proverbs were very interesting. When asked about the early bird catching the worm, he said there were two principles by which one could look at this proverb. The primary principle was that you would be able to beat your competition to your goals if you got going early, but the second principle was "a quality of birds that is compared to humans metamorphically" but said that he had to think about it before he could elaborate any further. Intellectual functioning is probably above average when thinking clearly.

Strengths and Assets: This is an intelligent youngster with a supportive family involved in outpatient therapy. He agrees to take the medication prescribed.

Diagnosis: This is a 16-year-old young man with a history of Attention-Deficit/Hyperactivity Disorder and depression who has become depressed over the last several months and now has a complicated delusional system which is being treated with medication. His aggressivity has decreased substantially, but the delusions persist. Therefore, the following diagnoses are given: Bipolar I Disorder, Mixed without Psychotic Features, and Attention-Deficit/Hyperactivity Disorder.

Recommendations: Hospitalization is indicated until mood is stabilized and reality testing has improved.   Pharmacological interventions were determined.

AUTHORS' COMMENTS: It is often difficult, especially in adolescents, to differentiate between Bipolar Disorder and Psychotic Disorders.   One of the areas for consideration is the presence or absence of prominent mood symptoms.   Although Matt presents delusional symptoms, he was given the Bipolar I diagnosis because of the presence of mood symptoms, specifically depression.

Dysthymic Disorder

This disorder is considered chronic, lasting at least 1 year for children and adolescents and at least 2 years for adults. It is characterized by disturbances in mood, such as depression or irritability, which are present most days for a large portion of the day.

This disorder is manifested by such symptoms as disruptions in sleeping and eating patterns, low energy level, lack of self-worth, feelings of inadequacy, difficulties in concentration and attention, lack of goal-directed behavior, difficulty with decision-making, and feelings of hopelessness. Children with this disorder may have difficulties with social relationships, reacting shyly or angrily towards peers and adults. School performance and occupational functioning may be adversely affected.

Because of its chronicity, children or adolescents with Dysthymic Disorder present a persistent pattern of impaired functioning and may not be easily recognized as experiencing psychological pain. When directly asked about their symptoms, children with Dysthymic Disorder may report that they have always been or felt "like this." Consequently, they tend to underreport their feelings and require a sensitive and probing interview in addition to information provided by others who know them well.

The difference between Dysthymic Disorder and Major Depressive Disorder is one of severity and duration. In Dysthymic Disorder, the symptoms are less severe, are less chronic, and have been present for at least 1 to 2 years, while in Major Depressive Disorder, symptoms are more acute and disabling, and their onset is more clearly determined. The difficulties in diagnosing Dysthymic Disorder relate to problems with determining the person's prior level of functioning with some degree of reliability because the individual may state, and others may report, that he or she has "always felt that way."

☑ CHECKLIST
DYSTHYMIC DISORDER

```
          +  Presence
   KEY    -  Absence
          *  Associated
             Feature
```

MAJOR SYMPTOMS:

*	Inattention
-	Impulsivity
*	Abnormal Activity Level
-	Aggressiveness
-	Violation of Rules
*	Isolation/Withdrawal/Avoidance
*	Inability to Form/Maintain Relationships
+	Disturbances of Affect/Mood
-	Anxiety
+	Depression
-	Delusions/Hallucinations
*	Somatic Complaints
-	Oddities of Behavior
-	Language Impairment
-	Impaired Cognition
+	Significant Distress/Impairment in Important Areas of Functioning

CASE SUMMARY

DYSTHYMIC DISORDER
Larry, C.A. 11–0

Presenting Problem: Larry is an 11-year-old referred for evaluation because of concerns about his social skills, self-image, and acting-out behavior. He is in a small special education class because of moderate learning disabilities. The school reports that for at least 1½ years, he has been increasingly distractible and easily frustrated. He frequently loses his temper and "sets himself up for rejection" by peers and adults. Larry dislikes team sports and is not involved in extra-curricular peer activities. He has difficulty falling asleep and has numerous somatic complaints.

Upon examination, Larry appeared depressed with sad affect and much tearfulness. He was withdrawn and seemed extremely passive in his interactions with others. His interactions with peers have been increasingly conflicted, as he has instigated and provoked others. Larry is avoidant in discussing difficult issues and has trouble accepting responsibility for his actions. Personality testing suggests that he tends to externalize blame. His statements to the examiner indicated passivity, hopelessness, and lack of motivation to improve his relationships with peers and adults.

A recent intelligence test resulted in an average score with above average performance on selected subtests. The psychologist noted that Larry's overall Average IQ may be a low estimate of his potential because of distractibility and lack of effort. Signs of depression were noted in his testing behavior as well as in the content of some of the responses.

In summary, Larry is a child of at least average intellectual potential who appears sad, seems anxious, has low self-esteem, and is easily overwhelmed by the social and emotional demands placed on him.

Diagnosis: A diagnosis of Dysthymic Disorder is made with recommendations for intensive therapeutic intervention for Larry and his family.

AUTHORS' COMMENTS: The chronicity of Larry's depressive symptoms justifies a diagnosis of Dysthymic Disorder. He presents many of the characteristics associated with this disorder, such as low self-image, irritability, sadness, poor social relationships, and marginal academic progress. Larry has been functioning within this general pattern for more than a year, precluding the existence of one or more discrete or specific Major Depressive Episodes.

Cyclothymic Disorder

This disorder is considered chronic, lasting at least 1 year for children and adolescents and at least 2 years for adults. It is characterized by unstable moods, at times including symptoms associated with depression and at other times including symptoms associated with hypomania. The severity of symptoms is not sufficient to meet the criteria for either a Major Depressive Episode or a Manic Episode.

☑ CHECKLIST

CYCLOTHYMIC DISORDER

```
        +  Presence
KEY     -  Absence
        *  Associated
           Feature
```

MAJOR SYMPTOMS:

*	Inattention
+	Impulsivity
+	Abnormal Activity Level
-	Aggressiveness
-	Violation of Rules
*	Isolation/Withdrawal/Avoidance
-	Inability to Form/Maintain Relationships
+	Disturbances of Affect/Mood
-	Anxiety
+	Depression
-	Delusions/Hallucinations
*	Somatic Complaints
-	Oddities of Behavior
-	Language Impairment
-	Impaired Cognition
+	Significant Distress/Impairment in Important Areas of Functioning

CASE SUMMARY
MAJOR DEPRESSIVE DISORDER, OPPOSITIONAL DEFIANT DISORDER, ATTENTION-DEFICIT/ HYPERACTIVITY DISORDER, DYSTHYMIC DISORDER
Doug, C.A. 14–2

Presenting Problem: This is one of multiple psychiatric hospital admissions for Doug, a 14-year-old adolescent who was brought to the emergency room following an apparent and impulsive suicide attempt with 40-plus vitamin C tablets with an intention to die. Doug has a longstanding history of depression, diagnosed as Dysthymic Disorder, Attention-Deficit/ Hyperactivity Disorder, and enuresis; he has been feeling quite hopeless and helpless, and increasingly depressed and irritable over the last 5 months. He has been fighting increasingly at home and at school, has been assaultive towards mother and peers, and has had numerous suspensions from school leading to increased depressive symptoms, anger, and the above-mentioned suicide attempt. Doug denies any suicidality at present, and claims that this apparently was an attempt to get into the hospital to be with his friends who are in the hospital. Doug denies any psychotic symptoms or any manic or hypomanic symptomatology.

Mental Status Examination: Doug is a 14-year-old, casually dressed, tearful, and depressed adolescent. He was quite cooperative but tearful throughout the interview. Psychomotor functioning shows moderate retardation. His speech is average. His affect was blunted. Mood was depressed, irritable, and somewhat nervous. He reports difficulty falling asleep, with decreased appetite but no apparent weight loss. He also reports increased anger, irritability, mood lability, and explosive aggressive outbursts. He denied current suicidal or homicidal ideations. There was no apparent thought disorder. He denied any hallucinations or delusions. There was mild anxiety with apprehensive expectation and hypervigilance. He denied any phobias, obsessions, compulsions, or fire-setting fascination.

Diagnosis: This is one of multiple psychiatric hospital admissions for this 14-year-old adolescent now coming to treatment because of depression with neurovegetative symptoms, aggressive acting-out behavior, and a recent overdose suicide attempt. Doug has been previously diagnosed with Dysthymic Disorder, Oppositional Defiant Disorder, and Attention-Deficit/ Hyperactivity Disorder. Given the presenting complaints, an additional diagnosis of Major Depressive Disorder is indicated.

Recommendations: Hospitalization is recommended because patient is clearly in danger of harming self. Pharmacological interventions were determined. Doug will be discharged when mood is stable, when there is absence of suicidality, when there is improved anger management and impulse control, and when firm aftercare plans are established.

AUTHORS' COMMENTS: Doug's case summary briefly mentions a long-term past history of depression and acting-out behavior. The diagnosis of Dysthymic Disorder refers to this long-term pattern of depressed mood. Although Doug denied suicidal ideation at the time of the examination, his most recent visit to the emergency room was due to an attempt to end his life by taking pills. This gesture, as well as his tearfulness and overall blunted affect during the psychiatric interview, indicates a more significant deression, thus warranting the additional diagnosis of Major Depressive Disorder. His disruptive and increasingly aggressive behaviors would indicate the presence of either an Oppositional Defiant Disorder or a Conduct Disorder.

ADJUSTMENT
DISORDERS

ADJUSTMENT DISORDERS

Changes in the *DSM-IV* include the regrouping of Adjustment Disorder with Withdrawal, Physical Complaints, and Work or Academic Inhibition into one subtype named *Adjustment Disorder, Unspecified Type.* The *DSM-IV* also addresses the duration of this disorder by proposing two specifiers: *Acute* and *Chronic.* The Acute specifier is used if the symptoms are present for less than 6 months after the stressful event. The Chronic specifier is used if the stressor or symptoms last 6 months or longer.

Adjustment Disorder involves psychological distress and impairment of overall functioning, such as school or social activity, due to an excessive, maladaptive reaction occurring within 3 months of the onset of a stressful event. In normal responses to stressful situations, individuals tend to overreact and then recover. Individuals with an Adjustment Disorder continue to be significantly affected and do not return to their previous level of functioning without intervention. This intervention may involve either the removal of the given stressor(s) or assistance in developing coping mechanisms.

Stressors may be single or multiple, recurrent or continuous. Some stressors are associated with developmental stages such as the onset of adolescence; others may be associated with situational difficulties such as changing schools, neighborhoods, and so on. Stressors may involve familial events such as parental conflict, divorce, illness, or arrival of a newborn sibling. Other events that may affect individuals or entire communities include natural disasters or societal strife such as racial or religious prejudice.

Vulnerability to any stressor depends on the psychological makeup of the individual. Some are severely affected by a mild stressor and may even be suicidal, while others only experience mild adjustment disorders in the presence of significant stressors.

To arrive at a diagnosis of Adjustment Disorder, school personnel or other professionals need to be particularly careful in identifying the premorbid functioning of the child and the particular stressful event(s) triggering the change in behavior. Lack of such information may lead to an erroneous diagnosis of Mood Disorders, Conduct Disorders, or Anxiety Disorders.

There are several subtypes of Adjustment Disorders depending on the predominant symptoms at the time of referral:

♦ **Adjustment Disorder with Depressed Mood:** Predominant symptoms include depressed mood, hopelessness, and tearfulness.

♦ **Adjustment Disorder with Anxiety:** Predominant symptoms include worry, nervousness, and jitteriness. In children, it may manifest itself with symptoms closely resembling Separation Anxiety Disorder.

♦ **Adjustment Disorder with Mixed Anxiety and Depressed Mood:** Predominant symptoms include a combination of depressive and anxious features.

♦ **Adjustment Disorder with Disturbance of Conduct:** Predominant symptoms include violation of the rights of others or of age-appropriate societal norms and rules. In children, it may resemble Conduct Disorder.

♦ **Adjustment Disorder with Mixed Disturbance of Emotions and Conduct:** Predominant symptoms include various combinations of depression and anxiety, as well as disturbance of conduct.

♦ **Adjustment Disorder, Unspecified:** In this subtype, a broader combination of symptoms may result from the psychosocial stressor(s). These may include social withdrawal from previously adequate social functioning; physiological complaints such as fatigue, headaches, and other aches and pains; and inability to work or function academically when previous performance was appropriate, such as difficulty completing homework or classwork assignments due to distress.

Table of Contents for
Adjustment Disorders

☑ CHECKLIST

ADJUSTMENT DISORDER WITH DEPRESSED MOOD

KEY	+	Presence
	-	Absence
	*	Associated Feature

MAJOR SYMPTOMS:

*	Inattention
-	Impulsivity
*	Abnormal Activity Level
-	Aggressiveness
-	Violation of Rules
-	Isolation/Withdrawal/Avoidance
*	Inability to Form/Maintain Relationships
+	Disturbances of Affect/Mood
-	Anxiety
+	Depression
-	Delusions/Hallucinations
-	Somatic Complaints
-	Oddities of Behavior
-	Language Impairment
-	Impaired Cognition
+	Significant Distress/Impairment in Important Areas of Functioning

☑ CHECKLIST

ADJUSTMENT DISORDER
WITH ANXIETY

KEY	+	Presence
	-	Absence
	*	Associated Feature

MAJOR SYMPTOMS:

*	Inattention
-	Impulsivity
-	Abnormal Activity Level
-	Aggressiveness
-	Violation of Rules
-	Isolation/Withdrawal/Avoidance
*	Inability to Form/Maintain Relationships
+	Disturbances of Affect/Mood
+	Anxiety
-	Depression
-	Delusions/Hallucinations
-	Somatic Complaints
-	Oddities of Behavior
-	Language Impairment
-	Impaired Cognition
+	Significant Distress/Impairment in Important Areas of Functioning

☑ CHECKLIST

ADJUSTMENT DISORDER WITH MIXED ANXIETY AND DEPRESSED MOOD

KEY	+	Presence
	-	Absence
	*	Associated Feature

MAJOR SYMPTOMS:

*	Inattention
-	Impulsivity
*	Abnormal Activity Level
-	Aggressiveness
-	Violation of Rules
-	Isolation/Withdrawal/Avoidance
*	Inability to Form/Maintain Relationships
+	Disturbances of Affect/Mood
+	Anxiety
+	Depression
-	Delusions/Hallucinations
-	Somatic Complaints
-	Oddities of Behavior
-	Language Impairment
-	Impaired Cognition
+	Significant Distress/Impairment in Important Areas of Functioning

☑ CHECKLIST

ADJUSTMENT DISORDER WITH DISTURBANCE OF CONDUCT

KEY		
	+	Presence
	-	Absence
	*	Associated Feature

MAJOR SYMPTOMS:

*	Inattention
*	Impulsivity
-	Abnormal Activity Level
*	Aggressiveness
+	Violation of Rules
-	Isolation/Withdrawal/Avoidance
*	Inability to Form/Maintain Relationships
-	Disturbances of Affect/Mood
-	Anxiety
-	Depression
-	Delusions/Hallucinations
-	Somatic Complaints
-	Oddities of Behavior
-	Language Impairment
-	Impaired Cognition
+	Significant Distress/Impairment in Important Areas of Functioning

☑ CHECKLIST

ADJUSTMENT DISORDER WITH MIXED DISTURBANCE OF EMOTIONS AND CONDUCT

KEY		
	+	Presence
	-	Absence
	*	Associated Feature

MAJOR SYMPTOMS:

*	Inattention
*	Impulsivity
-	Abnormal Activity Level
*	Aggressiveness
+	Violation of Rules
-	Isolation/Withdrawal/Avoidance
*	Inability to Form/Maintain Relationships
+	Disturbances of Affect/Mood
*	Anxiety
*	Depression
-	Delusions/Hallucinations
-	Somatic Complaints
-	Oddities of Behavior
-	Language Impairment
-	Impaired Cognition
+	Significant Distress/Impairment in Important Areas of Functioning

GENERAL INTERVIEW FORM

ADJUSTMENT DISORDERS

1. Within the past 3 months, has the child been exposed to one or more significant stressful events?   ☐ Yes ☐ No Describe.

2. Is there evidence of significant impairment in school, social, or occupational functioning?   ☐ Yes ☐ No

3. Are the child's reactions excessive and/or uncommon given the particular stressor(s)?   ☐ Yes ☐ No

4. Has the child shown a similar behavior pattern prior to the event(s)?   ☐ Yes ☐ No

5. Does the child have a long-term tendency to overreact to stressful situations?   ☐ Yes ☐ No

6. For how long have these symptoms been evident? Describe.

7. Has the child previously been diagnosed as having another mental disorder?   ☐ Yes ☐ No

CASE SUMMARY

ADJUSTMENT DISORDER
Carl, C.A. 13–1

Reason for Referral: Carl was referred because of an abrupt change in his behavior 4 months ago. He was always a restless, somewhat rebellious child in the classroom, but recently his behavior has deteriorated significantly. He now becomes agitated at minimal provocation, has been throwing things, and tried to strangle one of his peers.

Interview with Parents: Both parents attended this interview. We talked about mother's injuries; she was injured at work, treated at an intensive care unit, and seen by many neurologists. She had a subdural hematoma which was surgically treated. Following this, she developed a seizure, was placed on medication at the hospital, and then was released. Sometime later she discontinued medication and subsequently had another seizure. Mother admitted that she had become depressed due to a massive weight gain since the injury. She saw a psychiatrist, was hospitalized, and is currently taking anticonvulsive medication. Mother admitted that she was still depressed over her failure to lose weight. Neither parent seemed able to talk to Carl very effectively. Both of them were at a loss to understand his behavioral deterioration.

Interview with Carl: At first Carl denied any knowledge of stress at home, but he gradually became more verbal. He had witnessed his mother's original seizure and had been terrified. Carl described in detail how she began to shake, reached out for him, bit her tongue (which bled), and had difficulties breathing. The boy was convinced that his mother was going to die. When she was initially hospitalized after her accident, Carl was aware that they had to "cut her head open and work on her brain." He was also aware of her second hospitalization with "bad nerves" and linked both incidents, becoming convinced that she was in mortal danger of dying.

Carl also spoke freely about conditions at home; his parents are always yelling at each other. According to him, this is nothing new, as they have been fighting with each other for years. He is scared that one of them is going to leave, and he spends his time worrying about this and about his mother's health.

Summary: Carl is obviously reacting to a number of stressors. He has developed persistent fear of his mother's dying based on inaccurate knowledge about seizures. Additionally, he is fearful of being abandoned by one or the other of his parents. Carl is a boy continually beset by worries, some of which can be resolved in counseling.

Diagnosis: Adjustment Disorder with Mixed Anxiety and Depressed Mood - Acute

Recommendations: Carl would benefit from a special education class for children with emotional problems, together with counseling intervention. Both parents should also receive counseling to help them work things out with Carl in a frank and open manner and to reassure Carl that he will not be abandoned by one or both of his parents. Reassurance about his mother's physical condition can only occur after Carl is provided with a thorough explanation of the nature and outcome of her seizure disorder.

AUTHORS' COMMENTS: Before the onset of this disorder, Carl was described as a rebellious child, but not to the extent and severity demonstrated by his current behavior. Although several stressors were identified, the one that probably precipitated his change in behavior was witnessing his mother's seizure, which he could not fully understand. Fear of abandonment (through death or separation) became a preoccupation for him to the point of impairing his academic and social functioning. Emotional features operating at this time include a high degree of anxiety, anger, and depression. Based on this information, Carl is experiencing an Adjustment Disorder with Mixed Anxiety and Depressed Mood. Because his abrupt change in behavior occurred less than 6 months ago, an Acute specifier was given.

PERVASIVE DEVELOPMENTAL DISORDERS

PERVASIVE DEVELOPMENTAL DISORDERS

In the *DSM-III-R* this category of disorders included Autistic Disorder and Pervasive Developmental Disorder Not Otherwise Specified. The *DSM-IV* category of Pervasive Developmental Disorder includes five disorders: Autistic Disorder, Rett's Disorder, Childhood Disintegrative Disorder, Asperger's Disorder, and Pervasive Developmental Disorder Not Otherwise Specified.

All the above disorders involve some degree of impairment in social interaction, language/communication, and/or peculiarities in behavior, interests, and activities. Rett's Disorder and Childhood Disintegrative Disorder are characterized by normal early development, followed by a deterioration of functioning.

PERVASIVE DEVELOPMENTAL DISORDER AND SCHIZOPHRENIA

The *DSM-IV* has organized the multiplicity of symptoms found in Schizophrenia into two dimensions. The positive dimension refers to the distorted and excessive quality of typically normal behaviors, while the negative dimension reflects a decrement or loss of normal functioning. Symptoms in the positive dimension are delusions, hallucinations, disorganized speech, and disorganized or catatonic behavior. Symptoms in the negative dimension include flat affect, nonelaborative speech, lack of initiation, or lack of perseverance in goal-directed behavior.

The onset of Schizophrenia is more prevalent between the mid-teens and the mid-30s and follows a prior normal course of development. It is rarely diagnosed in children. Many of its symptoms, such as disorganized speech, peculiar behavior, disturbances in affect, and disturbances in interpersonal relatedness, can be accounted for by other childhood disorders, such as Autistic Disorder, or one of the other Pervasive Developmental Disorders.

The major difference between Schizophrenia and Pervasive Developmental Disorder is the presence or absence of delusions and hallucinations. If the presence of delusions and hallucinations can be clearly determined, then the diagnosis is more likely to be Schizophrenia or Autistic Disorder with Schizophrenia. In addition, children with Pervasive Developmental Disorder may exhibit a more profound impairment of affect and a more significant deficit in verbal expression.

AUTISTIC DISORDER

Behavioral characteristics of this disorder include the following: impairment in social interaction, in verbal and nonverbal communication, and in imaginative activity, and restricted repertoire of activities and interests.

Qualitative Impairment in Reciprocal Social Interaction

Children with this disorder have a history of failure to form attachments. Their lack of interest in people is first noted during infancy. This is usually demonstrated by minimal eye contact, unresponsiveness, or aversion to cuddling, affection, and physical contact. In addition, children with Autistic Disorder do not use social cues, such as facial expressions, body postures, or other nonverbal behaviors appropriately, nor can they interpret them accurately in others. There is a failure to develop cooperative, imaginative play or social friendships. For example, these children do not initiate contact with others for the purposes of sharing their feelings or interests, nor do they show empathy and awareness for the feelings and activities of others. Depending upon the degree of impairment and age, these children may eventually demonstrate some social interests. However, this is considered a shallow attempt and does not reflect true social interaction and reciprocity.

Qualitative Impairment in Verbal and Nonverbal Communication and Imaginative Activity

Absence or significant delays in verbal language occur in children with this disorder. If language is present, these children show echolalia, unusual speech melodies, lack of abstract terms, poor syntactic structure, word meanings usually known only to themselves, and difficulties in naming familiar objects. There is also a marked inability to use language in order to initiate and maintain a dialogue with another person. In older individuals with this disorder, there is an inability to comprehend jokes, irony, and double meanings. Usually, children and adolescents with Autistic Disorder do not attempt to compensate for their language deficits through nonverbal means such as gesturing, pointing, or imitating.

In the area of imaginative activity, children with this disorder lack the type of flexible, make-believe play requiring fantasy and imagination. When playing, they are observed engaging in the same repetitive activities without change or variety.

Markedly Restricted Repertoire of Activities and Interests

Abnormal responses to the environment can take many forms: The child may resist minor changes and be obsessively interested in specific objects, music, movement, or parts of the body. For example, the child may react violently to a simple change in routine, such as change of placement of a toy or a change in the sequence of dressing or washing. An excessive attachment to such unusual objects as buttons and rubber bands, or obsessive attraction to a specific sound may also be observed. In addition, repetitive and peculiar motor movements such as hand clapping, twirling, and spinning are often seen in children with this disorder.

Other Features

Behaviors associated with Autistic Disorder may include self-mutilation or other self-damaging actions, such as biting, head banging, or the like. Parents may report unusual patterns of eating, sleeping, and drinking (e.g., a self-limiting diet or a child's excessive fluid intake may be observed). These children have frequent and unexplainable mood changes, ranging from laughing to crying. There is an apparent lack of sensitivity or oversensitivity to such sensory stimuli as light, sound, or pain. They often seem unaware of such possible dangers as heights or street traffic, or they may become overly fearful and tense when encountering innocuous objects or events.

Significant delays in cognitive skills are evident in this syndrome. If testable, these children show better performance on manipulative tasks as opposed to abstract, verbal abilities. Some children may have an unusually good memory for isolated information, retained over several years. Despite the presence of higher level scatter skills, many of these children test in the Moderate to Severe range of mental retardation.

Long-range outcomes for children with this disorder depend on the degree of development of their verbal communication skills and intellectual abilities. A higher level of skill development is associated with better adaptability and more autonomy in later life.

Autistic Disorder may be associated with several other medical conditions, such as phenylketonuria, fragile X syndrome, anoxia during birth, encephalitis, maternal rubella, and infantile seizures.

Table of Contents for Autistic Disorder

☑ CHECKLIST

AUTISTIC DISORDER

KEY	+	Presence
	-	Absence
	*	Associated Feature

MAJOR SYMPTOMS:

*	Inattention
*	Impulsivity
*	Abnormal Activity Level
-	Aggressiveness
-	Violation of Rules
+	Isolation/Withdrawal/Avoidance
+	Inability to Form/Maintain Relationships
+	Disturbances of Affect/Mood
-	Anxiety
-	Depression
-	Delusions/Hallucinations
-	Somatic Complaints
+	Oddities of Behavior
+	Language Impairment
+	Impaired Cognition
+	Significant Distress/Impairment in Important Areas of Functioning

CASE SUMMARY
AUTISTIC DISORDER
Gary, C.A. 6–0

Reason for Referral: Gary's parents initiated the referral and requested an unbiased opinion of Gary's problems. Information from other sources, except neurological and audiological examinations, was not available to the present examiner.

Background Information: Gary, the oldest of two children, was born weighing 6 pounds, 9 ounces, by Caesarean section, without any maternal problems except for some mild toxemic symptoms. His mother described her pregnancy with Gary as a very difficult one. She was under the care of a physician for the entire time and experienced frequent nausea, dizziness, blackouts, and high blood pressure. She was hospitalized at 5 months, at which time she felt physicians were indicating that she might wish to consider a voluntary abortion. She refused to think of that possibility and continued through the pregnancy.

From birth to the age of 3 months, there were some serious feeding problems. Gary vomited frequently. He was not gaining weight and was unable to keep his feedings down. Gary never slept much as an infant; as a result, his parents also found it difficult to sleep. He was never on a schedule, which was very aggravating to his mother.

When he was 2 years of age, things settled down somewhat, and Gary went on to more of a routine. Developmental milestones in some areas were unremarkable. Gary was sitting with help between 4 and 5 months, and alone at 6 months. He never crawled but went from sitting to walking with help at 10 months, and alone at 12 months. He was toilet trained for daytime at about 3½ years; at night he is still not bladder trained. His mother had great difficulty in training Gary and managed only because she "kept after him constantly."

Gary was babbling at 6 months of age. He stopped making sounds a few weeks before his first birthday. He made no more sounds until he was about 3 to 3½ years old. There were never any single recognizable words, combined words, or sentences.

Gary is not interested in looking at books, except to rip them, nor has he any interest in being read to.

Developmentally, his mother feels that some days Gary seems to do things "normally" with the exception of speech. Other days, and these are most of the time, he has some problems following directions, amusing himself, and functioning in matters of daily living.

Health History: As a small baby, Gary was always sick with colds, fever, earaches, or "something." He had a high fever, and from the description it sounds as though there was a convulsion. Until the age of 2 or 2½, he had frequent ear infections and running ears. A recent audiological examination ruled out any hearing impairment.

Parents report that Gary's favorite activities are playing on his swings, finger painting, and cutting with scissors. He makes his needs known mostly by helping himself to whatever he desires. For example, if he wants a drink and someone else has a drink of something on the table, he will take that other person's glass and drink from it. When he can't explain himself or make his needs known, he gets terribly frustrated and will kick and throw things.

During examination, some activity with his fingers was noted, which his parents later explained as starting when attempts were made to begin teaching him sign language. Prior to that time, Gary showed no unusual finger concentration.

Psychological Assessment: Gary's interactions with people and objects have been extremely limited. He has numerous toys but seldom plays with them. He enjoys swings and will, on occasion, watch one or two cartoons on television. Gary appears to have limited awareness of his 17-month-old sibling and will often push him out of his way or just walk into him.

According to his parents, when Gary was approximately 3 years of age, he said, "I want a drink." This was the first and last sentence they heard. He will occasionally say "mommy" when in distress but generally emits numerous unspecific sounds.

Gary has frequent temper tantrums whenever he is frustrated at obtaining something he wants, engages in lengthy staring spells while rocking, and spends considerable time tearing the pages of books. Also reported and evidenced throughout the evaluation was ritualistic, compulsive finger play.

Gary withdrew when he initially met the examiner. His contact, such as holding hands while walking to the test room, was marked by indifference or almost total lack of awareness of people or surroundings. Impulsivity predominated throughout the evaluation session. Gary was unable to focus on any material or use it adaptively. He moved from object to object without using them meaningfully.

Gary's limited exploration of materials was at a very primitive level. He would smell materials presented to him, then put them down and begin engaging in finger posturing. When further attempts were made to have him investigate materials, he would often place them in his mouth. Hand puppets were presented, but they did not elicit appropriate behavior. Although there was an increase in the sounds he made, he generally pushed the puppets away or bit their heads.

Attempts to have Gary carry out commands proved futile for the most part. However, on two occasions he was able to follow through when demands were repeated at a rapid pace. At these times, however, there was a noticeable increase in his activity level, finger posturing, and the appearance of spinning behavior. Gary twirled himself around as he approached the object he was asked to obtain.

Impressions: Gary demonstrated gross and sustained impairment of emotional relationships with people. He is unaware of his own personal identity. He appears to have little or no regard for the accepted function of objects in his environment and demonstrates a sustained resistance to change. Speech appears to have been acquired but then lost, and his parents cite numerous developmental problems. All of these behaviors are indicative of Autistic Disorder. I suggest that approaches to Gary and his development be modeled after those used with autistic children.

Diagnosis: Autistic Disorder

AUTHORS' COMMENTS: With respect to qualitative impairment in reciprocal social interaction, Gary shows significant lack of awareness of people and his surroundings with almost no responsivity towards them.

Language development, if in fact it occurred at all, is currently reduced to unspecific sounds and does not appear related to any attempts at communication. Additionally, there is little evidence of imaginative play, as demonstrated by his inability to creatively use puppets and other toys.

Gary evidences rocking, spinning, twirling, finger concentration, and other ritualistic behaviors symptomatic of restricted activities and interests. His inability to respond appropriately involves such behaviors as book ripping, grabbing items from others, and not responding to any requests.

An audiological examination ruled out hearing loss, which might have contributed to delayed language acquisition. A formal psychological evaluation could not be completed due to Gary's lack of responsivity; he smelled the test materials and placed them in his mouth. Given these behaviors, and the degree and severity of Gary's impairment, the diagnosis of Autistic Disorder has been appropriately made.

CASE SUMMARY
AUTISTIC DISORDER
Charles, C.A. 3–1

Reason for Referral: Charles was seen for a developmental evaluation regarding the possibility of a diagnosis of a sociocommunicative disorder based on concerns his parents and physician have had about his development. He has a history of absent speech with echolalia (he taps at his mouth when hungry, but not clearly with communicative intent), likes to run back and forth, has poor social skills, has an insistence on some routines, has a lack of play (with a strong interest in hangers), and has a lack of response to certain sounds without true evidence of a hearing impairment. Charles has been in good health in general. He was evaluated as an infant for possible progressive macrocephaly and a febrile seizure. Both an EEG and cranial ultrasound studies were normal. Charles was delivered by Caesarean section and weighed 8 pounds and 5 ounces. There were no difficulties in the postnatal period.

Charles' parents first became concerned at his lack of language by around 2½ years of age though on review, he was not a cuddly child and may have had some unusual interests and activities. While Charles does respond to some direct commands, these often have gestures associated with them. His use of eye contact is limited and not particularly communicative, and he shows minimal, if any, communicative intent with sound or gesture and still uses non-speech-based sounds. He does not yet demonstrate any emerging representational play and still shows unusual interests (his fascination with hangers, and today he was putting tissues in his mouth, and seemed to enjoy spitting). He does not seem interested in play near or with others and prefers solitary pursuits or occasional roughhouse play with adults (especially his parents).

Diagnosis: Using observation and semistructured play activities as well as his history and formal diagnostic instruments, a diagnosis of Autistic Disorder was able to be confirmed at this time. His temperament and echolalia are relative strengths, but he does show the requisite behaviors in all cardinal areas.

Charles has no true expressive language (he uses words rarely and inconsistently) and his receptive skills are similarly delayed or lacking (though he seems to have learned to focus on just a few words rather than using any larger linguistic concepts). He continues to have a large amount of jargon and random sound production. His oromotor functions appear normal.

Charles has relatively few early social skills; he also has intense interest without developing any pretend play or imitation, and a frequent display of repetitive behaviors and motor stereotypes. Accordingly, he shows the requisite alterations in the cardinal areas of communication, socialization, and play to permit a clear diagnosis of Autistic Disorder at this time.

Recommendations: In general, Charles' programming should address his socialization and his communication skills explicitly with clear goals established. I would recommend that this be done as much as possible in an environment that would support incidental as well as explicit learning. At present, communication is his most urgent need. As an aside, the use of physical activity may enhance both socialization and communication so that letting Charles be active may enhance his learning a particular "lesson." Communication programming might benefit from the use of total communication techniques (the use of speech, signing, and pictures or object-miniatures) to enhance the chance of Charles' understanding the message and of catching his interest.

Supportive services should include special education, communication (not limited to classic speech therapy), and occupational therapy.

At this point, Charles is showing significant needs in most areas. However, long-range predictions (either medical or educational) cannot be clearly made at this point, and I would suggest that formal norm-based testing be deferred for about 2 to 3 years. The use of criteria-based testing may be helpful to the school and the parents in arriving at a description of Charles' levels of function in a variety of areas.

From a medical standpoint I have recommended two tests: these are genetic studies on blood and are now generally felt to be routine in children with autism though they are positive in only a small percentage of cases. The first is a fragile X study by DNA analysis; the second a routine chromosome study. In addition, I suggest that formal audiological assessment be done to confirm adequate hearing for speech acquisition and to observe for hyperacusis as well.

Charles' parents have been given materials regarding national, regional, and local services as well as lists of books to serve as resources.

AUTHORS' COMMENTS: Charles' evaluation addressed the major areas associated with a diagnosis of Autistic Disorder: language and communication, social interaction, repertoire of activities and interests. Included in the case study were peculiar behaviors and unusual interests, particular to Charles. Medical recommendations to rule out fragile X syndrome and chromosomal abnormalities as well as hearing acuity and sensitivity follow usual diagnostic procedures for children with autism.

Testing issues were well addressed in that it is not always possible to use normative instruments with children who display such severe problems in language, communication, attention, and social interaction.

RETT'S DISORDER

Rett's Disorder is present only in females. One of its most prominent features involves a regression in head growth between the ages of 5 and 48 months. After developing normally for approximately 5 months, children with this disorder show significant regression in specific psychomotor skills, such as fine and gross motor coordination. Subsequently, hand movements become increasingly stereotypical rather than purposeful and may resemble gestures of hand washing or hand wringing. Gross motor impairment is demonstrated by awkward body movements and difficulties walking smoothly. As early as the preschool years, these children may show an indifference to their environment, similar to those with Autistic Disorder. However, in Rett's Disorder, social interactions tend to develop and improve over time. Speech and language development are also significantly impaired. Intellectual assessment usually places these children at the Severe or Profound range of Mental Retardation.

☑ CHECKLIST
RETT'S DISORDER

	+	Presence
KEY	-	Absence
	*	Associated Feature

MAJOR SYMPTOMS:

-	Inattention
-	Impulsivity
-	Abnormal Activity Level
-	Aggressiveness
-	Violation of Rules
*	Isolation/Withdrawal/Avoidance
+	Inability to Form/Maintain Relationships
-	Disturbances of Affect/Mood
-	Anxiety
-	Depression
-	Delusions/Hallucinations
-	Somatic Complaints
+	Oddities of Behavior
+	Language Impairment
+	Impaired Cognition
+	Significant Distress/Impairment in Important Areas of Functioning

CASE SUMMARY
RETT'S DISORDER
Rose, C.A. 15–6

Reason for Referral: Rose was referred for reevaluation because of recent concerns about her deterioration in functioning. She was previously diagnosed as severely autistic and has received special education since 3 years of age.

Rose's parents describe her as having been a healthy baby who had no feeding problems. She sat unsupported at 8 months of age, crawled at a normal time, and walked at 13 months of age. Her parents stated that at 1 year of age, Rose was "perfectly normal." She did not play with toys but did have a toy rabbit that she carried about. Between 1 and 2 years old, Rose wore "braces" for intoeing. She cooed and gurgled but never spoke any words. She did, however, scream loudly and regularly. At age 2, Rose's pediatrician raised the possibility of autism, and Rose was evaluated and diagnosed as being severely autistic. She had onset of petit mal seizures 3 or 4 years ago and has not yet started menarche.

Prior to 1 year of age, Rose began exhibiting head-banging behavior, which persists. At roughly the same time, she began exhibiting hand wringing, which her parents describe as being essentially constant during her waking hours. Rose currently has episodes of breath-holding as well as hyperventilation. She is ambulatory; however, her parents feel that her walking has deteriorated markedly in the past 5 years and expressed concern at her toe-walking. They noted that, if left standing, Rose ultimately will begin to walk on her own with difficulty. They also noted that if, for example, a cookie was left on the table, Rose would ultimately use her hands to scoop the cookie into her mouth. However, she otherwise has minimal use of her hands. On initial questioning, Rose's parents did not recall any unusual coolness of Rose's feet; however, during the interview they did remark that Rose often does seem to have cold and blue feet. They further stated that Rose's abdomen often appears bloated. A full physical examination has been completed and the results put in her file. Of note are findings that Rose's measured head circumference is significantly below the 50th percentile for her age group.

Impressions and Recommendations: Rose is a 15½-year-old female with mental retardation, autistic features, and short stature. She impressed the examiner as an alert-appearing female who seemed unaware of her surroundings. She exhibits several of the criteria associated with Rett's Disorder, specifically, female sex; normal pre- and perinatal period with essentially normal psychomotor development through the first 6 months of life; early behavioral, social, and psychomotor regression with evolving communication dysfunction; loss of purposeful hand use through age 1 to 4 years; and hand wringing. She also exhibits gait apraxia. Rose presents a number of associated clinical features of Rett's Disorder, including hyperventilation/breath-holding, seizures, hyperreflexia, short stature, vasomotor instability of the feet, and abdominal bloating.

AUTHORS' COMMENTS: Rose has many of the typical features associated with Rett's Disorder. Although her parents described her as "perfectly normal" as an infant, she showed significant regression in psychomotor skills, increased stereotypical hand movements, and difficulties walking smoothly as she developed. Rose does not use language for communication except for cooing and gurgling. One of the more important features of this disorder involves a decrease in head growth, which was reported in Rose's case. It was difficult to explore her level of social interaction since Rose presents as a significantly retarded adolescent with many autistic features.

CHILDHOOD DISINTEGRATIVE DISORDER

The major difference between Autistic Disorder and Childhood Disintegrative Disorder is the age of onset of symptoms. In Childhood Disintegrative Disorder, there is a period of normal development for at least the first 2 years of life before a marked deterioration in at least two of the following areas of functioning appears: expressive or receptive language, social skills or self-help skills, bowel or bladder control, ability to play, and/or motor skills.

In addition, there is abnormal functioning in at least two of the areas associated with Autistic Disorder: social interaction, verbal and nonverbal communication, imaginative play, and repertoire of activities and interests.

The abrupt changes that occur in the child's development may be preceded by a different set of symptoms. These may include high activity levels, restlessness, anxiety, and a loss of speech skills. Intellectual abilities of children with this disorder are usually in the mentally retarded range.

☑ CHECKLIST

CHILDHOOD DISINTEGRATIVE DISORDER

KEY	+ Presence - Absence * Associated Feature

MAJOR SYMPTOMS:

*	Inattention
*	Impulsivity
*	Abnormal Activity Level
-	Aggressiveness
-	Violation of Rules
*	Isolation/Withdrawal/Avoidance
+	Inability to Form/Maintain Relationships
+	Disturbances of Affect/Mood
-	Anxiety
-	Depression
-	Delusions/Hallucinations
-	Somatic Complaints
+	Oddities of Behavior
+	Language Impairment
+	Impaired Cognition
+	Significant Distress/Impairment in Important Areas of Functioning

CASE SUMMARY

CHILDHOOD DISINTEGRATIVE DISORDER
Dwayne, C.A. 3–3

Reason for Referral: Dwayne was referred for evaluation because of parental concerns about his present functioning. According to them, he was born after an unremarkable pregnancy and delivery and was described as a very alert baby, responsive to touch, sound, and movement. Dwayne was a good eater and sleeper and was a fun-loving baby who brought a great deal of joy to his parents.

Dwayne's mother returned to work when he was 7 months of age and became pregnant again when he was 20 months of age. Dwayne easily established strong bonds with his caretaker at the day care setting, and all other areas of development continued to progress normally. His parents reported that as a toddler, Dwayne had many words, loved to look at books, and easily engaged in interactive play.

At about 23 months of age, Dwayne had a series of respiratory infections, necessitating frequent medications. At the same time, his parents noticed that Dwayne was becoming increasingly anxious, experiencing frequent nightmares and daytime fears of unfamiliar people. When his sister was born, Dwayne cried uncontrollably and tried to hurt her several times. He was no longer interested in playing with his toys or looking at his books and spent most of his time "spaced out," according to his parents. Of great concern was Dwayne's lack of verbal communication as compared to his numerous words spoken previously. When not "spaced out," he would run around aimlessly, waving his hands and shouting. The parents took Dwayne for a full medical examination, which resulted in negative findings.

Psychiatrist's Evaluation: When Dwayne came for the assessment, he looked briefly at, and then quickly away from, the examiner, walking around the room without any sense of purpose or direction. There was little interaction between Dwayne and his parents while all three were together in the room. He was able to follow a few parental commands, but responded with either noises or gestures as opposed to any words. After a few minutes, he pointed to a dish of lollipops in the room and waited until one was offered to him. The lollipop seemed to calm Dwayne down for a while as he sat more quietly in his chair. When given a toy, he placed it on the floor, ignored it, and instead, roamed around the room in a clumsy and unfocused manner.

Diagnosis: Given Dwayne's early history of being a verbal, alert, and playful boy, the current picture indicates a significant decline from previous functioning. He does not verbalize in a meaningful way, has limited social relatedness, and shows no imaginative play. Childhood Disintegrative Disorder is probably the most appropriate diagnosis at this time.

AUTHORS' COMMENTS: This case illustrates the abrupt changes in functioning from a normally developing child to one who no longer has verbal communication skills, has limited social interactions, and has no apparent interest in activities. Of note are his parents' descriptions of Dwayne's high anxiety levels, increased activity, and frequent crying, which preceded the current symptoms observed at the time of evaluation.

ASPERGER'S DISORDER

Unlike Autistic Disorder, children who are diagnosed with Asperger's Disorder have age-appropriate language, self-help skills, and cognitive development. Like Autistic Disorder, there is a marked impairment in reciprocal social interactions and a restricted repertoire of behaviors, interests, and activities. These children usually misread nonverbal cues and are unable to share with others. They seem to lack the empathy and reciprocity necessary to develop normal peer relationships. In general, they show a deficiency in understanding the subtleties of social rules which manage behavior. In addition, they may demonstrate stereotyped motor movements, fixation on parts of objects, limited interests, and specific but purposeless routines.

In the early years, children with Asperger's Disorder may appear clumsy and poorly coordinated, and may have difficulties with writing tasks. In school, they may excel at tasks requiring good rote memory, such as facts and information about the few subjects in which they are intensely interested. Despite apparent knowledge about a particular subject, they lack understanding of the facts they have acquired. Although they often have a large vocabulary, the content of their speech and writing tends to be primitive and inappropriately applied. Because of their peculiarities and poor social interaction skills, these children may become the targets of much teasing and bullying.

Of all the Pervasive Developmental Disorders, Asperger's Disorder results in the least impairment in overall functioning. Because these children may be aware of their own differences and peculiarities, they may be more emotionally fragile.

Table of Contents for Asperger's Disorder

☑ CHECKLIST
ASPERGER'S DISORDER

KEY	
+	Presence
-	Absence
*	Associated Feature

MAJOR SYMPTOMS:

*	Inattention
*	Impulsivity
*	Abnormal Activity Level
-	Aggressiveness
-	Violation of Rules
+	Isolation/Withdrawal/Avoidance
+	Inability to Form/Maintain Relationships
+	Disturbances of Affect/Mood
-	Anxiety
-	Depression
-	Delusions/Hallucinations
-	Somatic Complaints
+	Oddities of Behavior
*	Language Impairment
*	Impaired Cognition
+	Significant Distress/Impairment in Important Areas of Functioning

CASE SUMMARY
ASPERGER'S DISORDER
Simone, C.A. 5–3

Reason for Referral: Simone was referred for evaluation by her parents and her pediatrician who had concerns about her pattern of difficulties. While she is a bright child, attending a private nursery school, she tells long stories to herself, demonstrates poor eye contact, has difficulty relating to other children, and seems different from other children her age. She has a history of parroting what others say and did not learn to ask "why?" until recently when taught by her mother. Simone has had low muscle tone since infancy and has been seen for neurological assessment. She was also noted to have a large head. Muscle enzyme studies were done and reported as normal.

Simone was seen over the course of 6 hours. She was attended by her parents, who provided much of the information. Simone was felt to be in her usual state of health and to have behaved in a representative fashion.

By history, Simone has been generally healthy. She was the product of a 37-week planned pregnancy. Delivery was by stat Caesarean section for distress. She did well initially but developed some unspecified complications and spent her first night in the special care nursery. Mother had a postpartum depression for a few months, late in Simone's first year. The pediatrician noted motor delays in Simone, and this matched fears that mother had regarding Simone's development compared to other children. This is when a neurologist was consulted and the mildly low tone was noted. Physical therapy was recommended. Simone is on no chronic medications or regimens, and has no history of traumatic loss of consciousness or seizures or hospitalizations after birth. A current physical examination was noncontributory and did not suggest any specific underlying syndrome.

Simone showed an improvement in tone over the next year and walked by 15 months but was felt to have difficulties with attention and interaction. Testing and enrollment in a nursery school for contact with other children was suggested. Her first words came at around 14 to 15 months. Simone was felt to have improved with enrollment in nursery school, and there were few concerns. However, over time, Simone has displayed distinct personality traits that have resulted in this referral. She notices small changes in her environment, such as if a drawer is slightly open, though she does not notice other things. She tells long stories mixing elements from favorite TV shows and movies and shows clear interest in interaction, especially with other children. More recently, it seems as if Simone uses language less spontaneously than others her own age. She only urinates at home and shows a fear of toilets. She repeats rules and phrases and seems to have an advanced memory for such things as places and directions. She refuses to do certain things but is generally flexible; it is not clear if some of her refusals represent "can't" or "won't." Simone is felt to have trouble with transitions though she does better if she is prepped. She has no rituals or particularly unusual movements or attachments. On review, she does like mirrors and will sometimes look at items out of the corner of her eye. She likes to make silly rhymes and seems creative and self-sufficient. She is felt to do better in small rather than large groups and does well with one or two children if she knows them well. Her interactions with others, eye contact, and sociability have all improved over the last few years.

On evaluation, Simone showed no evidence of true shyness. She interacted relatively well though she did demonstrate what I felt might be marginally overly precise speech. She showed an excellent memory for rote items and was easygoing throughout the day. Her comments were often tangential, however, and required parental interpretation. In addition, her language and interpretation were concrete though she showed excellent receptive and expressive skill levels. She did not attempt to initiate engagements but was generally passive. She did demonstrate some echolalia and showed excellent articulation. Simone demonstrated an understanding of the concepts of real versus make believe and showed no impairment of reality testing.

Diagnosis: Using observation as well as semistructured interviews and parent reports, a diagnosis of Asperger's Disorder was identified. Due to her high level of abilities in many areas, she does not fulfill criteria for a diagnosis of classic autism, as per the *DSM-IV* or the Childhood Autism Rating Scale. While Simone clearly has high intelligence and very good abilities, she does demonstrate the requisite alterations in the three cardinal areas necessary for diagnosis. Her communication is overly precise and pedantic, and her nonverbal communication, including gesture and facial expression, is not as skilled as one would expect. Her social skills are marked by an interest in interaction hampered by the inability to read social cues or modify her behavior effectively without a great deal of work. Her interests and routines are generally appropriate, but investigation suggests that her somewhat rote play as well as her interest in rules and facts and her selective resistance in certain areas are explained by this diagnostic category. Long-term implications are more difficult, however. Simone has been generally successful in school but is showing increasing difficulties with the work and with relating to classmates. The application of a label may be more detrimental than helpful if she shows major improvements in the near future. There is the distinct possibility that to consider her eccentric, or like someone who "marches to the beat of a different drummer" may be just as appropriate. The use of a diagnostic label of Asperger's Disorder may then be thought of as more useful to her family in working through what adaptations they must make to help Simone maximize her potential.

The preceding findings were reviewed with Simone's parents at the time of the evaluation. In addition, they were shown copies of a newsletter and an information book regarding individuals with high-level abilities who have sociocommunicative difficulties. It is not clear if Simone will need major alterations to her academic program though she may require the addition of programming in upper level pragmatics and socialization skills. Attention should be paid to difficulties in interpretation and synthesis which would be expected to occur; Simone has good language skills, but they may be concrete. I reviewed with the parents that Simone's behavior and comments will generally have meaning though these may be tangential, and that interpretation and determination of her level of comprehension may be difficult for others to understand. I also suggested that talking about feelings and describing to Simone what feelings she seems to be displaying may be helpful to her in understanding herself and others. Giving her choices, rather than asking for spontaneous selection, may also be helpful in the near future, especially when she seems inattentive or confused.

Long-term implications are not possible at present. Simone skirts the border between children who may just be different and those who do have more specific needs. Time (over the next few years) will probably tell, and the resources mentioned earlier will be helpful. Formal testing by the school system should be interpreted with care; Simone's rote skills may be misleading, and she may have more difficulty than is initially appreciated with verbal interpretations. Attention to semantics, pragmatics, and social skills should be explicit if an Individualized Educational Plan is developed.

AUTHORS' COMMENTS: This case illustrates many of the behaviors associated with Asperger's Disorder. Although Simone has well-developed language skills, her ability to interact verbally is characteristically different. She seems to have difficulties interpreting social cues, responds in a tangential manner, and displays a concrete quality in her language use.

Simone demonstrated strong rote memory skills and an interest in factual data; however, she could not integrate them with higher level thinking and reasoning. Because of her young age, it is difficult to predict the impact that her behaviors will have on her overall school and social functioning as the demands and expectations of these environments increase.

GENERAL INTERVIEW FORM
PERVASIVE DEVELOPMENTAL DISORDERS

The following questions have been separated into the three major symptom categories described previously: Qualitative Impairment in Reciprocal Social Interaction; Qualitative Impairment in Verbal and Nonverbal Communication and Imaginative Activity; and Markedly Restricted Repertoire of Activities and Interests. Additional questions are included to help the reader differentiate among the four Pervasive Developmental Disorders described previously.

Qualitative Impairment in Reciprocal Social Interaction

1. Does the child show significant lack of awareness of the existence or feelings of others?   ☐ Yes ☐ No

2. How does the child seek comfort when ill, hurt, or tired? Describe.

3. Does the child imitate normal routines of others?
    ☐ Yes ☐ No   Describe.

4. Does the child participate in social play activities at age-appropriate levels?   ☐ Yes ☐ No

5. Does the child understand the rules and conventions of social interaction?   ☐ Yes ☐ No

Qualitative Impairment in Verbal and Nonverbal Communication and Imaginative Play

6. Does the child use age-appropriate communication skills, such as babbling, facial expressions, mimicking, or spoken language?   ☐ Yes ☐ No

7. Does the child use age-appropriate nonverbal communication, such as eye gaze, facial expression, body posture, and general gestures to initiate or respond to interaction? ☐ Yes ☐ No

8. Does the child engage in imaginative activities such as using fantasy, play acting, or imaginary characters? ☐ Yes ☐ No

9. Does the child have peculiarities of speech, such as lack of variety in tone of voice, inappropriate pitch and volume, or statements ending in question-like melodies? ☐ Yes ☐ No

10. Does the child show significant impairment in speech form and content, such as echolalia, repetitive use of speech, inappropriate use of pronouns, or irrelevancy of subject matter?   ☐ Yes ☐ No

11. Does the child show significant impairment in his or her ability to initiate conversation and maintain dialogue? ☐ Yes ☐ No

Markedly Restricted Repertoire of Activities and Interests

12. Does the child show odd motor movements, such as unusual hand/finger movements, spinning, walking on tiptoes, or head banging?   ☐ Yes ☐ No

13. Is the child overly preoccupied with smells, parts of objects, textures of things, or spinning wheels of toy cars; or is he or she overly attached to uncommon objects, such as string or rubber bands?   ☐ Yes ☐ No

14. Is the child unable to cope with minor everyday changes in the environment? ☐ Yes ☐ No

15. Does the child have a compulsive need to do things in the same manner every day? ☐ Yes ☐ No

16. Does the child show a restricted range of interests; for instance, interest only in lining up objects, collecting facts about one subject, or pretending to be exclusively and repeatedly one imaginary character? ☐ Yes ☐ No

17. Is the child over- or undersensitive to such stimuli as sound or light? ☐ Yes ☐ No

18. Does the child experience mood swings, such as unexplained crying, giggling, or laughing? ☐ Yes ☐ No

19. Does the child respond appropriately to real dangers in the environment, such as traffic or heights? ☐ Yes ☐ No

20. At what age were the above characteristics first noticed? Describe.

21. Has the child experienced delusions or hallucinations? ☐ Yes ☐ No

Deterioration from Previous Status or Functioning

22. Was the child born with a normal head size? ☐ Yes ☐ No   If yes, was there a deceleration of head circumference during infancy?

23. Has the child lost previously acquired gross-motor skills? ☐ Yes ☐ No   If yes, at what age? Describe.

24. Has the child lost previously acquired fine-motor skills?
☐ Yes ☐ No   If yes, at what age? Describe.

25. At what age did the child achieve bladder control? Has the child been able to maintain control?   ☐ Yes ☐ No Describe.

26. At what age did the child achieve bowel control? Has the child been able to maintain control?   ☐ Yes ☐ No Describe.

27. Has the child's ability and interest in play decreased significantly from previously attained levels?
☐ Yes ☐ No

FEEDING AND EATING DISORDERS

FEEDING AND EATING DISORDERS

The *DSM-IV* presents a new category of Eating Disorders specifically associated with infancy or early childhood. Included in this section are Pica, Rumination Disorder, and Feeding Disorder of Infancy or Early Childhood. In the *DSM-III-R,* these disorders were part of the general category of Eating Disorders, which also included Anorexia Nervosa and Bulimia Nervosa.

PICA

The *DSM-IV* adds additional criteria for the diagnosis of Pica. It considers the developmental level of the child and his or her cultural background regarding the ingestion of non-nutritive substances.

This disorder is characterized by the intake of nonfood substances when there is no aversion to common foods. Infants usually ingest paint, plaster, hair, cloth, or string. Older children may eat bugs, sand, leaves, droppings, or stones. Adolescents and adults may ingest dirt or clay but also can easily eat regular foods. The most common physical complications of this disorder are lead poisoning, associated with paint intake, and intestinal obstructions as a result of ingestion of foreign objects. Deficiencies in certain minerals (iron, zinc), poor parental supervision, and mental retardation may be associated with this disorder.

Because infants (up to 18 months of age) often attempt to eat nonfood substances, the diagnosis of Pica should be given only when the behavior is not typical for a child's developmental level and is present for at least 1 month.

Table of Contents
for Pica

☑ CHECKLIST
PICA

```
         +  Presence
KEY      -  Absence
         *  Associated
            Feature
```

MAJOR SYMPTOMS:

-	Inattention
-	Impulsivity
-	Abnormal Activity Level
-	Aggressiveness
-	Violation of Rules
-	Isolation/Withdrawal/Avoidance
-	Inability to Form/Maintain Relationships
-	Disturbances of Affect/Mood
-	Anxiety
-	Depression
-	Delusions/Hallucinations
-	Somatic Complaints
+	Oddities of Behavior
-	Language Impairment
*	Impaired Cognition
-	Significant Distress/Impairment in Important Areas of Functioning

INTERVIEW FORM

PICA

1. Does the child engage in persistent eating of nonfood substances? ☐ Yes ☐ No   Describe.

2. For how long has this pattern been observed? Describe.

3. Has this pattern of ingesting nonfoods persisted beyond the ages of 18 to 24 months?   ☐ Yes ☐ No

4. Is the child interested in consuming appropriate food substances?   ☐ Yes ☐ No

5. If consumption of paint has occurred, has the child been examined recently by a physician for lead poisoning?
☐ Yes ☐ No

6. Is there adequate supervision at home?   ☐ Yes ☐ No

CASE SUMMARY

PICA

Beth, C.A. 6–3; Susan, C.A. 4–5

Reason for Referral: A medical report was received by the school as a result of developmental assessments and follow-up for both girls.

Beth and Susan are half-sisters who are being followed medically because of their past history of lead poisoning. An initial diagnosis of lead poisoning was made on the basis of routine blood screening when Beth was 2½ years and Susan was 6 months old. At the time the blood was tested, Beth was irritable and had a decreased appetite, and Susan was failing to thrive.

The children lived with their mother in an older, multifamily house, which had a high lead level in the paint on the bathroom walls and on the window sills. Both children are noted to pick up nonfood items and consume them.

The children were admitted to the hospital for treatment on three occasions over 7 months. Current developmental assessment indicates significant concerns about their language development, distractibility, and short attention span with recommendations for special school placement.

AUTHORS' COMMENTS: This case illustrates a long-term pattern of eating nonfood substances. Ingesting paint with high lead content resulted in harmful consequences both physically and cognitively.

RUMINATION DISORDER

Infants with this disorder convey the impression of considerable pleasure from repeated regurgitation of partially digested food. Usually the food is released from the mouth or chewed and swallowed again. Nausea, gastrointestinal pain, and rejection of food do not accompany this disorder. Its onset occurs after a period of normal food intake. Between episodes of throwing up, the infant may display signs of irritability usually associated with hunger.

This disorder can be life threatening because of weight loss or malnutrition. Reactions to stress in the child's environment, lack of stimulation by the caretaker, and/or difficulties between parent and child may precipitate this disorder. As a result of the infant's behavior, the primary caretaker may feel discouraged in the attempts to feed the baby and may become passive, avoid the child, and refrain from normal stimulation. If the disorder is not successfully treated, delays in all aspects of the child's development may occur.

☑ CHECKLIST

RUMINATION DISORDER

```
        + Presence
KEY     - Absence
        * Associated
          Feature
```

MAJOR SYMPTOMS:

-	Inattention
-	Impulsivity
-	Abnormal Activity Level
-	Aggressiveness
-	Violation of Rules
-	Isolation/Withdrawal/Avoidance
-	Inability to Form/Maintain Relationships
-	Disturbances of Affect/Mood
-	Anxiety
-	Depression
-	Delusions/Hallucinations
-	Somatic Complaints
+	Oddities of Behavior
-	Language Impairment
*	Impaired Cognition
-	Significant Distress/Impairment in Important Areas of Functioning

INTERVIEW FORM

RUMINATION DISORDER

1. Does the infant engage in the repeated regurgitation of foods, not preceded by nausea, retching, or disgust?
    ☐ Yes ☐ No

2. For how long has this behavior been observed? Describe.

3. Has the child been eating normally before these episodes appeared?   ☐ Yes ☐ No

4. Has the child experienced weight loss or failure to gain expected weight for his or her developmental age?
    ☐ Yes ☐ No

5. Is this behavior associated with a physical disorder?
    ☐ Yes ☐ No

6. How has the caretaker been affected by the infant's periods of repeated regurgitation? Describe.

7. Are any developmental delays suspected?
    ☐ Yes ☐ No

CASE SUMMARY

RUMINATION DISORDER

Penny, C.A. 6 Months

Reason for Referral: Penny was admitted to the hospital for evaluation because of failure to thrive. She was the product of a full-term, uncomplicated pregnancy, with normal labor and delivery. At birth, she weighed 6½ pounds, was in good condition, and had no difficulties in the neonatal period. She was initially breast fed.

At 8 weeks, because of Penny's vomiting, her mother changed her to formula feeding. The vomiting continued in spite of numerous formula changes, and at 6 months of age she weighed only 9 pounds. Medical evaluation found no pathology other than esophagitis secondary to vomiting. Penny was observed to induce vomiting either by her hands or by tongue thrusting.

Treatment focused on directing Penny's interpersonal stimulation outward. This necessitated a 3-week hospital stay during which nursing, psychological, and occupational therapists worked intensively with Penny and her mother.

AUTHORS' COMMENTS: This case clearly illustrates the pattern of Rumination Disorder. In such cases, a complete developmental evaluation is indicated to rule out delays in other areas of the infant's functioning brought about by the lack of food retention.

FEEDING DISORDER OF INFANCY OR EARLY CHILDHOOD

This is a new disorder for the *DSM-IV,* not previously included in the *DSM-III-R.* It involves a significant failure to gain weight or a significant weight loss because of failure to ingest food adequately. Infants typically have some difficulties with feeding, but children with this disorder have persistent problems (more than 1 month duration), may become irritable during feeding, cannot easily be soothed, seem passive, are uninvolved in the feeding, and may suffer from developmental delays. The infant's feeding problems are not due to a specific or general medical condition. The lack of nutritional intake may affect the child's mood and/or ability to develop normally, which can, in turn, perpetuate feeding problems.

Conditions which may be associated with this disorder are parental instability, child abuse or neglect, or developmental impairments.

☑ CHECKLIST
FEEDING DISORDER OF INFANCY OR EARLY CHILDHOOD

	+ Presence
KEY	- Absence
	* Associated Feature

MAJOR SYMPTOMS:

-	Inattention
-	Impulsivity
*	Abnormal Activity Level
-	Aggressiveness
-	Violation of Rules
*	Isolation/Withdrawal/Avoidance
*	Inability to Form/Maintain Relationships
-	Disturbances of Affect/Mood
-	Anxiety
-	Depression
-	Delusions/Hallucinations
-	Somatic Complaints
-	Oddities of Behavior
*	Language Impairment
*	Impaired Cognition
-	Significant Distress/Impairment in Important Areas of Functioning

INTERVIEW FORM
FEEDING DISORDER OF INFANCY OR EARLY CHILDHOOD

1. Has the child failed to gain expected weight or lost significant weight for his or her age and size?
   ☐ Yes ☐ No

2. Describe the child's feeding behaviors.

3. Has a medical condition been ruled out as the cause of feeding problems?   ☐ Yes ☐ No

4. Does the child show normal alertness, curiosity, and interest in his or her environment?   ☐ Yes ☐ No

5. Does the child convey emotions through vocalizations, gestures, or facial expressions?   ☐ Yes ☐ No

6. Is there evidence of physical abuse, or emotional or physical neglect?   ☐ Yes ☐ No   If yes, describe.

CASE SUMMARY
FEEDING DISORDER OF INFANCY OR EARLY CHILDHOOD
Peter, C.A. 3–2

Reason for Referral: Peter was brought to the attention of the pediatrician by a neighbor who was concerned about seeing the boy unattended for a long period of time.

Upon examination, the child was found to be grossly underweight, unresponsive, and physically neglected. His cry was noted to be weak, with overall poor motility. Peter seemed apathetic and unwilling or unable to respond verbally to the pediatrician. He did not explore any toys available in the office.

Further investigation revealed a young single mother with no family support in the area. She was very depressed and felt lonely and unable to care for her child, whom she described as "difficult to handle," especially during feeding times. She herself, had been adopted after spending most of her childhood in several different foster placements.

Peter was hospitalized to treat his failure to thrive. A social worker met with the mother and convinced her to join a parenting group. Within a month, Peter physically began to thrive; he also showed increasing alertness and social interest. Both Peter and his mother are being monitored by a social agency.

Diagnosis: A diagnosis of Feeding Disorder of Infancy or Early Childhood was made.

AUTHORS' COMMENTS: Peter shows many of the symptoms associated with this disorder. He was difficult during feeding times, appeared uncommunicative, and was obviously weak and underweight because of the lack of nutritional intake. In addition, his physical and emotional needs were further compromised by a mother who was alone, depressed, and frustrated with her son's feeding difficulties.

EATING DISORDERS

There are minor changes in the criteria for the diagnoses of Anorexia Nervosa and Bulimia Nervosa from the *DSM-III-R* to the *DSM-IV.* In Anorexia Nervosa, two subtypes have been defined: *Restricting Type* and *Binge-Eating/Purging Type.* Two subtypes have also been defined in Bulimia Nervosa, according to the presence or absence of the purging behavior.

ANOREXIA NERVOSA

Anorexia Nervosa is characterized by either a significant weight loss or inability to reach the expected weight, given the individual's age and height (85% according to medical norms). In both cases, there is a refusal to sustain appropriate body weight, intense fear of becoming obese, severe body image distortion, and depending upon physical maturity level, amenorrhea in females. Fear of gaining weight results in reduction of food intake, self-induced vomiting, use of laxatives, and prolonged bouts of physical exercise.

Individuals with Anorexia Nervosa show a marked preoccupation with body size and shape; they tend to scrutinize themselves in an obsessive manner, never believing they are thin enough. Their self-esteem is closely tied to the belief that weight loss is a form of self-control and discipline, while weight gain is perceived as a lack of self-control. Self-referral for treatment of Anorexia Nervosa is rare because these individuals tend to deny or are unaware of the severity of their condition.

Psychological symptoms may include depression, difficulty in socialization, blunt affect, sleep problems, and moodiness. Obsessive-compulsive behaviors are common, especially around the subject of food.

Subtypes presented in *DSM-IV* include the Restricting Type and the Binge-Eating/Purging Type. In the Restricting Type, the individual loses weight or fails to gain expected weight by depriving himself/herself of food and engaging in frequent and intense exercise. In the Binge-Eating/Purging Type, the individual ingests food but will then employ methods to get rid of it, such as induced vomiting, enemas, and so forth.

☑ CHECKLIST

ANOREXIA NERVOSA

KEY	+	Presence
	-	Absence
	*	Associated Feature

MAJOR SYMPTOMS:

-	Inattention
-	Impulsivity
-	Abnormal Activity Level
-	Aggressiveness
-	Violation of Rules
*	Isolation/Withdrawal/Avoidance
-	Inability to Form/Maintain Relationships
-	Disturbances of Affect/Mood
-	Anxiety
-	Depression
-	Delusions/Hallucinations
+	Somatic Complaints
+	Oddities of Behavior
-	Language Impairment
-	Impaired Cognition
*	Significant Distress/Impairment in Important Areas of Functioning

INTERVIEW FORM
ANOREXIA NERVOSA

1. Does the person express intense fear of being obese in contrast to his or her actual body weight?
   ☐ Yes ☐ No

2. Does the person complain of feeling fat while his or her weight is normal?   ☐ Yes ☐ No

3. Does the person fail to reach or refuse to maintain minimal body weight for age and height?   ☐ Yes ☐ No

4. How much weight has the person lost? Describe.

5. Has a recent medical examination ruled out physical causes for the weight loss?   ☐ Yes ☐ No

6. In females, has there been any disruption in the menstrual cycles?   ☐ Yes ☐ No

7. Does the person acknowledge or realize that his or her behavior is abnormal?   ☐ Yes ☐ No

8. Does the person engage in excessive use of laxatives or self-induced vomiting to get rid of ingested food?
   ☐ Yes ☐ No

9. Does the person severely restrict or deprive himself or herself of food?   ☐ Yes ☐ No

10. Does the person engage in intense exercise in order to lose weight?   ☐ Yes ☐ No

11. Describe any unusual behaviors associated with food, such as limiting intake to only low-caloric foods, binge eating, hoarding, concealment, and throwing food away.

12. Is the person overly preoccupied with his or her body image; for instance, frequently staring at a full-length mirror, stating dissatisfaction with specific body parts? ☐ Yes ☐ No

13. Is the person irritable, moody, or depressed? ☐ Yes ☐ No

14. Has there been a recent stressful event in the person's life? ☐ Yes ☐ No

15. Does the person engage in obsessive-compulsive or perfectionistic behaviors?   ☐ Yes ☐ No   Describe.

CASE SUMMARY

ANOREXIA NERVOSA, RESTRICTING TYPE
Nadia, C.A. 12–4

Reason for Referral: Nadia, a 12-year-old girl, was referred for hospitalization by her pediatrician because of a 17-pound weight loss over the past 3 months. She denied vomiting and diarrhea but had complained in the past of constipation. She had reduced her food and liquid intake markedly, which caused significant family stress. The family then forced her to eat. In spite of having dropped from the 50th to the 5th percentile in weight (for height), Nadia felt she was of normal weight. She was an honor student and immaculate housekeeper. All her friends are achievers, but she has recently become socially withdrawn. She is not and never has been very communicative with her parents.

Her past medical history is unremarkable. The family consists of her parents, both high school graduates, and their two daughters, Nadia being the elder. A new baby is expected in 2 months.

Nadia was begun on bed rest, with increasing privileges in response to weight gain. Calorie counts were maintained. She was seen for daily psychotherapy while an inpatient. It was felt that her eating disorder was the response to the stresses of impending adolescence, coupled with the anticipated changes in her family constellation by the birth of the new sibling. Nadia was hospitalized for 6 weeks, then discharged to continue outpatient therapy. Although she continued to be overly preoccupied with food intake, she was able to maintain weight within normal limits for her height and age.

AUTHORS' COMMENTS: Nadia's loss of more than 15% of her body weight could not be accounted for by any medical condition. She significantly reduced her own food intake, qualifying her as a Restricting Type of anorexic. Nadia denied that she was losing weight; attempts by the family to force food intake probably created more stress for her.

Children with this disorder are often described as high achievers and meticulous to the point of being compulsive. Another commonly found feature (which was apparent with Nadia) involves withdrawal from peer group activities.

Anorexia Nervosa may be precipitated by a stressor; in this case the onset of adolescence as well as the birth of a new sibling were the stressors identified by the psychologist.

BULIMIA NERVOSA

Bulimia Nervosa is characterized by binge eating followed by behaviors to offset the possibility of gaining weight. Binge eating involves the rapid consumption of large amounts of food, usually chosen for their sweet taste, high caloric content and form, which enables fast eating. Consumption is done secretly with limited chewing, in order to consume as much food as possible in the shortest amount of time.

In order to rid themselves of the food they have ingested, such individuals tend to engage in induced vomiting, overuse of laxatives or diuretics, and/or vigorous exercise. They also may resort to strict dieting or fasting.

In this disorder there is acknowledgment of abnormal eating patterns; fear of not being able to control eating; and accompanying depression, anxiety, and/or self-punishing statements or thoughts after unrestrained eating has occurred. In general, the person's life appears to be dominated by conflicts about eating and preoccupation with body weight and appearance. Because of the excessive value placed on body shape, individuals with Bulimia Nervosa tend to suffer from low self-esteem. Abuse of other substances, such as barbiturates, amphetamines, cocaine, or alcohol, may be present.

For those individuals who have routinely engaged in binging and purging behaviors, physical examination may reveal damage to the teeth, throat, and salivary glands, with additional gastric disturbances and possibly even heart problems.

Subtypes presented in the *DSM-IV* include *Purging Type* and *Nonpurging Type.* The first type always involves self-vomiting and other purging techniques, while the second type is considered when the individual usually resorts to other techniques in the attempt to control weight, such as excessive exercise, fasting, dieting, and so forth.

Table of Contents for
Bulimia Nervosa

☑ CHECKLIST
BULIMIA NERVOSA

KEY	+ Presence
	- Absence
	* Associated Feature

MAJOR SYMPTOMS:

-	Inattention
*	Impulsivity
-	Abnormal Activity Level
-	Aggressiveness
-	Violation of Rules
-	Isolation/Withdrawal/Avoidance
-	Inability to Form/Maintain Relationships
*	Disturbances of Affect/Mood
*	Anxiety
*	Depression
-	Delusions/Hallucinations
*	Somatic Complaints
+	Oddities of Behavior
-	Language Impairment
-	Impaired Cognition
-	Significant Distress/Impairment in Important Areas of Functioning

INTERVIEW FORM
BULIMIA NERVOSA

1.   Does the person engage in recurrent binge eating?
     ☐ Yes ☐ No

2.   Is the person aware that his or her eating pattern is abnormal, and is he or she fearful of not being able to control it?   ☐ Yes ☐ No

3.   Is there excessive use of purging behaviors, such as the use of laxatives, self-induced vomiting, and the use of diuretics, in attempts to lose weight?   ☐ Yes ☐ No

4.   Does the person engage in such nonpurging behaviors as severely restrictive diets or strenuous exercise in attempts to lose weight?   ☐ Yes ☐ No

5.   Is the person overly preoccupied with his or her body image?
     ☐ Yes ☐ No

6.   How often does the person engage in binging episodes? Describe.

7.   Is the binging behavior characterized by any of the following?

     ♦ Consumption of high-caloric, easily ingested foods
        ☐ Yes ☐ No

     ♦ Inconspicuous or secretive eating during a binge
        ☐ Yes ☐ No

     ♦ Termination of such eating episodes by sleep, abdominal pain, self-induced vomiting, or social interruption   ☐ Yes ☐ No

8.   Does the person appear depressed and/or express self-punishing thoughts following binge eating?
     ☐ Yes ☐ No

9.   Does he or she engage in abuse of substances, such as alcohol, cocaine, sedatives, or amphetamines?
     ☐ Yes ☐ No

CASE SUMMARY

BULIMIA NERVOSA, PURGING TYPE
Debbie, C.A. 16–2

Medical Findings: Debbie was initially seen by the school nurse, who referred her for further evaluation to a nearby clinic. She is a high school sophomore who was referred for medical care because of pain and swelling on the left side of her face. Detailed history was obtained. She had been overweight 4 years earlier and, under medical supervision, lost 24 pounds. She was now at approximately her ideal body weight. However, maintaining her weight was difficult. Debbie was very involved in exercise and used it for weight maintenance.

Eighteen months ago at Christmas, she began vomiting after large meals. The vomiting became more frequent and when she came in for evaluation, she was vomiting almost every day after meals. At first she denied the use of laxatives, emetics, diet pills, and diuretics but later admitted using laxatives and self-induced vomiting to control her weight.

Upon inquiry of her eating patterns, Debbie stated that she tends to ingest large quantities of food secretly, especially pizzas, cakes, and cookies. Following a binge, Debbie attempts to fast for several days. She expressed anger with herself for not being able to control these urges and admitted being overly preoccupied with food.

On physical examination, Debbie had swelling and tenderness of the left parotid, a salivary gland. She was pale and appeared unhealthy. She also lacked energy. Lab work revealed iron deficiency anemia. She was hospitalized to stabilize her medical condition and to begin family oriented therapy.

Diagnosis: A diagnosis of Bulimia Nervosa, Purging Type was made.

AUTHORS' COMMENTS: This case clearly illustrates the binge and purge pattern of Bulimia Nervosa, Purging Type, the psychological factors associated with it, and some of the physical consequences of this disorder.

ELIMINATION
DISORDERS

ELIMINATION DISORDERS

These disorders include Encopresis and Enuresis. They are included in this book because of their possible impact on a child's self-image and social functioning. Children with these disorders may suffer embarrassment, low self-esteem, and negative reactions such as anger, punishment, and rejection from caretakers. Impairment in social functioning may be characterized by avoidance of overnight activities, teasing, and ostracism from peers.

ENCOPRESIS

There are some changes in criteria for diagnosis of this disorder from the *DSM-III-R* to the *DSM-IV.* Duration of the disturbance has been shortened from 6 months to 3 months. The *DSM-IV* considers two subtypes of Encopresis: **With Constipation and Overflow Incontinence,** and **Without Constipation and Overflow Incontinence,** depending on the formation of feces and whether the soiling is continuous or sporadic. In the first subtype, constipation tends to be chronic; fecal matter is not well formed, but excretion is continuous and responsive to treatment for constipation. In the second subtype, there is no evidence of constipation. Fecal matter is of normal formation and excretion is sporadic. Because feces are left in conspicuous places, this subtype can be associated with oppositional or conduct problems.

This disorder involves involuntary, or in some cases intentional bowel movements, not due to the presence of a physical condition, and discharged in places other than the toilet, such as in clothing or on the floor. Especially when bowel movements are involuntary, constipation may occur because the child experiences anxiety about defecating in a specific place or refuses to defecate because of an overall pattern of oppositional behaviors. For such diagnosis to be made, children must be 4 years old or have a developmental level equivalent to 4 years of age. The episodes of Encopresis must occur at least once per month for at least 3 months in order to meet criteria.

This disorder may be precipitated by stressful events such as birth of a sibling or entering school. Intentional release of feces and/or smearing of feces may be associated with antisocial behavior.

Encopresis may be diagnosed in a child who has never achieved bowel continence or in one who has established continence and then develops a pattern of incontinence.

Table of Contents
for Encopresis

☑ CHECKLIST
ENCOPRESIS

```
        +  Presence
KEY     -  Absence
        *  Associated
           Feature
```

MAJOR SYMPTOMS:

-	Inattention
-	Impulsivity
-	Abnormal Activity Level
-	Aggressiveness
-	Violation of Rules
*	Isolation/Withdrawal/Avoidance
*	Inability to Form/Maintain Relationships
*	Disturbances of Affect/Mood
*	Anxiety
-	Depression
-	Delusions/Hallucinations
-	Somatic Complaints
+	Oddities of Behavior
-	Language Impairment
-	Impaired Cognition
*	Significant Distress/Impairment in Important Areas of Functioning

INTERVIEW FORM
ENCOPRESIS

1. Does the child defecate in inappropriate places?
   ☐ Yes ☐ No

2. If yes, how often does this occur? Describe.

3. What are the child's chronological and mental ages?

4. Has a recent medical examination ruled out physical causes for the Encopresis?   ☐ Yes ☐ No

5. Does the child feel embarrassed or does he or she avoid social situations as a result of this condition?
   ☐ Yes ☐ No

6. Has the child recently been under unusual stress such as birth of a sibling, hospitalization, or entering school?
   ☐ Yes ☐ No

7. Does the child become anxious when expected to defecate in a specific place?   ☐ Yes ☐ No

8. Is the child's defecation in inappropriate places a deliberate behavior?   ☐ Yes ☐ No

9. Does the child show any such oppositional or antisocial behaviors as excessive aggressiveness, temper tantrums, asociality, or destruction of property?   ☐ Yes ☐ No

10. Does the child suffer from constipation?   ☐ Yes ☐ No

11. What management techniques have been attempted by the caretakers to deal with the child's encopresis? Describe.

CASE SUMMARY
ENCOPRESIS
Jason, C.A. 7–9

Reason for Referral: Jason, a 7½-year-old boy, was admitted to the hospital for treatment of Encopresis as attempted outpatient management had failed. His family reported that he had never been successfully bowel trained.

Toilet training began shortly before the birth of a younger sibling when Jason was 2 years old. By age 4, he was continent of urine but not of stool. He normally soiled twice a day, before and after school. A gastroenterologist was consulted and the appropriate studies were done to rule out an organic cause.

When Jason was 6 years old, he was referred to a behavioral clinic. He was started on the usual regimen of cleansing enemas, stool softeners, and scheduled times on the toilet, with rewards for clean pants, bowel movements in the toilet, and complying with medication. He did well initially, using a star chart and trading in stars for material rewards. After acquiring cable TV as a reward, he quit taking the medication and complying with the chart system. Soiling resumed.

Jason was then begun on cleansing enemas, followed by stool softeners and a regular toileting schedule. A contract was agreed upon in which primary responsibility was placed on Jason. Bowel continence was promptly achieved.

A psychological evaluation was obtained because of the prolonged course of the disorder even with prior medical management. He was found to be in the superior range of measured intelligence. The personality assessment indicated withdrawal as his primary strategy. Jason indicated awareness of his needs but hesitation to seek fulfillment through others. He perceived closeness to others as associated with loss, and thus avoided involvement.

Because of these findings and observations of his tendency to withdraw while hospitalized, recommendations were made for individual and family psychotherapy. He was discharged after 2 weeks of combined medical and psychological management. On follow-up, Jason continued to be continent 1 year later.

AUTHORS' COMMENTS: Jason presents a long-term pattern of fecal incontinence since an early age. A medical examination ruled out physical causes for his incontinence. Because defecation was initially related to school (before and after), this was the apparent stressor. His tendency to avoid interaction with others may be considered a more revealing underlying cause for his Encopresis.

ENURESIS

The *DSM-IV* shortened the frequency between episodes of Enuresis but lengthened their duration: from two or more times per month in the *DSM-III-R* to twice a week for at least 3 consecutive months. If the latter criteria is not met, there must be at least a significant impact on social, academic, or other areas of functioning in order to meet the criteria for Enuresis. The *DSM-IV* considers three subtypes: *Nocturnal Only,* which occurs during the night; *Diurnal Only,* which occurs during the day; and *Nocturnal and Diurnal,* when the enuretic event occurs at both times.

This disorder involves the voiding of urine usually into clothing or in bed, beyond an age when such control would be expected (by age 5 or its equivalent developmental level). The repeated release of urine can be either intentional or unintentional. For such a diagnosis to be made, physical causes such as diabetes, urinary tract infection, or seizure disorder must be ruled out.

This disorder is relatively common and may be precipitated by stressful events such as birth of a sibling, entering school, or changing neighborhoods. Diurnal Enuresis tends to occur more often in females and may be due to hesitance to use public facilities, such as in school, friends' homes, or recreation areas.

Enuresis may be diagnosed in a child who has never achieved urinary continence (by age 5) or in one who has established it and then develops a pattern of incontinence (between ages 5 and 8 years).

☑ CHECKLIST
ENURESIS

	+ Presence
KEY	**- Absence**
	∗ Associated Feature

MAJOR SYMPTOMS:

-	Inattention
-	Impulsivity
-	Abnormal Activity Level
-	Aggressiveness
-	Violation of Rules
∗	Isolation/Withdrawal/Avoidance
∗	Inability to Form/Maintain Relationships
-	Disturbances of Affect/Mood
-	Anxiety
-	Depression
-	Delusions/Hallucinations
-	Somatic Complaints
+	Oddities of Behavior
-	Language Impairment
-	Impaired Cognition
∗	Significant Distress/Impairment in Important Areas of Functioning

INTERVIEW FORM
ENURESIS

1. Does the child show repeated voiding of urine during waking or sleeping times regardless of whether it is intentional or unintentional?   ☐ Yes ☐ No

2. When are these episodes most prevalent? Describe.

3. How often do these occur? Describe.

4. Has a recent medical examination ruled out physical causes for this behavior?   ☐ Yes ☐ No

5. What are the chronological and/or mental ages of the child?

6. Does the child feel embarrassed, or does he or she avoid social situations as a result of this condition?
    ☐ Yes ☐ No

7. Has the child recently been under unusual stress, such as the birth of a sibling, hospitalization, or entering school?
    ☐ Yes ☐ No

8. What management techniques have been attempted by the caretakers to control the child's voiding? Describe.

CASE SUMMARY

ENURESIS, NOCTURNAL ONLY
Harold, C.A. 8–2

Reason for Referral: Harold, an 8-year-old boy, was brought to the psychologist because his continued nightly bedwetting prevented him from sleeping at friends' homes or participating in overnight camping with the Cub Scouts. He and his family sought help as their attempts at managing his Enuresis (using after-dinner deprivation of liquids and awakening him in the late evening) did not work. The boy and his mother were having increasingly hostile interchanges over the wetting situation. He was dry during the day.

The medical history was not significant. Recent physical examination ruled out urinary tract infection and kidney dysfunction. Overall, Harold was developing normally and had been toilet trained easily by age 3. The onset of bedwetting had occurred 2 years before, coinciding with the birth of a sibling.

Harold was started on a conditioning system using a bell to awaken him when wetting began. He was also given the responsibility to change his pajamas and bedding. A reward system using a chart was initiated. Gradual improvement was noted as soon as 1 week. Three months were required before he felt secure enough to go away from home for an overnight trip. There was no relapse when the bell conditioning system was discontinued.

AUTHORS' COMMENTS: Harold shows repeated inability to control urination during the night. Referral was made because of the social implications of his voiding behaviors at home and away from home. A medical examination ruled out physical reasons for Harold's incontinence. Toilet training had been achieved at the expected developmental age. In Harold's case, Enuresis was most likely precipitated by the birth of a sibling. The diagnosis of Enuresis, Nocturnal Only is warranted.

SLEEP
DISORDERS

SLEEP DISORDERS

During the course of parental interviews, information concerning the child's sleep patterns may be reported to the mental health professional. Common parental complaints include nightmares and sleepwalking.

The following syndromes have been selected from a more comprehensive group of sleep disorders described in the *DSM-IV* because of their incidence and age of onset: Nightmare Disorder, Sleep Terror Disorder, and Sleepwalking Disorder. The two latter ones may occur concurrently.

NIGHTMARE DISORDER

Formerly Dream Anxiety Disorder, Nightmare Disorder is characterized by frequent sleep interruptions due to vivid dreams which are usually threatening and frightening to the child. Upon awakening, the child is oriented and alert, is able to recall the dream in detail, but becomes distressed by its content and is usually unable to go back to sleep. Common themes of such nightmares include threats to survival, security, or self-esteem. For example, a child may report recurrent nightmares with such content as bad people coming into the house to kill him and his family. His attempts to rescue his family fail because he was not quick enough to protect them. Another dream content may involve running away and failing to escape from monsters.

Nightmares are common during childhood, often beginning between the ages of 3 and 6 years. However, this problem is not considered a clinical disorder unless it causes sufficient distress and/or interferes to a significant degree with daily functioning. The fear of recurrent nightmares may cause the child to avoid going back to sleep. Interrupted sleep may also contribute to problems during the day, such as poor concentration, listlessness, fatigue, and feelings of depression and anxiety.

Nightmare episodes tend to occur during REM (rapid eye movement) sleep, and more often during the latter part of the night. Because this period of sleep inhibits body movement, parents do not usually notice physical signs of agitation in the child while he or she is dreaming. This disorder is more prevalent in children who have experienced a psychosocial stressor; it is not diagnosed as a separate syndrome if the nightmares are associated with Posttraumatic Stress Disorder. Therefore, the mental health professional should conduct a thorough investigation of the context in which these nightmares are occurring.

Table of Contents for
Nightmare Disorder

☑ CHECKLIST
NIGHTMARE DISORDER

```
        +  Presence
KEY     -  Absence
        *  Associated
           Feature
```

MAJOR SYMPTOMS:

-	Inattention
-	Impulsivity
-	Abnormal Activity Level
-	Aggressiveness
-	Violation of Rules
-	Isolation/Withdrawal/Avoidance
-	Inability to Form/Maintain Relationships
-	Disturbances of Affect/Mood
+	Anxiety
-	Depression
-	Delusions/Hallucinations
-	Somatic Complaints
-	Oddities of Behavior
-	Language Impairment
-	Impaired Cognition
+	Significant Distress/Impairment in Important Areas of Functioning

INTERVIEW FORM

NIGHTMARE DISORDER

1. Does the child exhibit repeated interruptions in sleep because of frightening dreams?   ☐ Yes ☐ No

2. What is the content of these dreams? Describe.

3. Describe the child's behavior upon awakening.

4. What time of night do the nightmares generally occur? Describe.

5. After awakening from a nightmare, can the child easily go back to sleep?   ☐ Yes ☐ No

6. Is the child taking medication?   ☐ Yes ☐ No
   If yes, what kind?

7. Has there been a recent stressful event in the child's life?
   ☐ Yes ☐ No

8. Does the child have a history of mental and/or physical health problems?   ☐ Yes ☐ No   Describe.

SLEEP TERROR
DISORDER

Sleep Terror Disorder is differentiated from Nightmare Disorder in that in Sleep Terror Disorder, there is a higher anxiety level, a tendency for the episode to occur earlier in the night, and usually no dream recall. Abrupt awakening usually begins with a panicky scream or yell; behaviors during the event may include physiological symptoms such as perspiration, dilated pupils, and rapid pulse. Also present are motor movements such as hitting the air or trying to get out of the bed to flee, which may cause injury to the child or to those in close proximity. The Sleep Terror episode may also involve a frightened facial expression, an increase in anxiety, and an overall agitated state. Children with this disorder do not respond to, or actively resist, attempts at communication or comfort from others. Some of the physical characteristics present during Sleep Terror incidents also occur during Seizure Disorder, but one difference may be that in the latter, the episodes may also manifest themselves during waking hours. However, Seizure Disorder and Sleep Terror Disorder can take place concurrently.

Sleep Terror episodes may last from 1 to 10 minutes, and occur during non-REM sleep, usually during the first part of the night. With younger children, there may be a vague sensation of panic immediately upon awakening from the nightmare. Older children and adolescents may recall some terrifying images from the dream. But in all cases, there is no recollection of the Sleep Terror occurrence by the next morning.

This problem is not considered a clinical disorder unless it causes sufficient distress and/or interferes to a significant degree with social or occupational functioning. Social impairment may occur because of reluctance to go on overnight visits, such as to camp or with friends. Strained parent-child interactions may occur because of disruptions to the home life. Interruptions in sleep may affect the child's functioning in the school setting.

Although recurrent Sleep Terror episodes are only experienced by 1% to 6% of children, isolated episodes appear to be more common. They seem to be related to a familial history of sleep disturbances and may be precipitated by stress, febrile illness, excessive fatigue, and/or bedtime medication.

Table of Contents for
Sleep Terror Disorder

☑ CHECKLIST

SLEEP TERROR
DISORDER

	+ Presence
KEY	- Absence
	* Associated Feature

MAJOR SYMPTOMS:

-	Inattention
-	Impulsivity
-	Abnormal Activity Level
-	Aggressiveness
-	Violation of Rules
*	Isolation/Withdrawal/Avoidance
-	Inability to Form/Maintain Relationships
-	Disturbances of Affect/Mood
+	Anxiety
-	Depression
-	Delusions/Hallucinations
+	Somatic Complaints
-	Oddities of Behavior
-	Language Impairment
-	Impaired Cognition
+	Significant Distress/Impairment in Important Areas of Functioning

INTERVIEW FORM
SLEEP TERROR DISORDER

1. For how long has the child been asleep before the onset of the episode? Describe.

2. Describe the child's behavior during the sleep disturbance.

3. How long does the episode last?

4. Does the child remember the episode in the morning?
   ☐ Yes ☐ No

5. Describe the child's responses to attempts at arousal.

6. Does the child suffer from seizures or Central Nervous System complications?   ☐ Yes ☐ No

7. Is there a familial history of sleep disturbances?
   ☐ Yes ☐ No

8. Has the child recently been under stress or overly fatigued?
   ☐ Yes ☐ No

9. Is the child taking medication?   ☐ Yes ☐ No
   If yes, what kind, and when is it taken?

CASE SUMMARY

SLEEP TERROR DISORDER
Jane, C.A. 4–2

Reason for Referral: Jane, a 4-year-old girl, was brought to the pediatrician because of extremely severe nightmares. For about 6 weeks she had been awakening three to four times a week screaming. This usually occurred in the late evening while the parents were still awake. Her parents would rush into her room each time and attempt to determine the reason for her screams. The child was very difficult to engage and unable to say why she was troubled. Usually, after a few minutes with her parents she would resume sleep. Jane had no other unpredictable episodic behaviors for the remainder of the night. The next morning she would not recall the incident. There was no unusual stress or discernible significant trauma in the recent past.

Jane was completely normal upon examination. She was felt to have a simple Sleep Terror Disorder. Valium on a low dosage was prescribed for 2 weeks, with gradual withdrawal from the medication after that. The episodes ceased and did not recur.

AUTHORS' COMMENTS: Jane's nightmares occurred several hours after going to sleep. She woke up screaming and was unable to be aroused by her parents during the episode. Jane could not recall the incident the next morning. Other than her screaming, Jane's physical manifestations during the episodes were not described. Duration of each episode was not reported.

One of the differences between Sleep Terror and Nightmare Disorder is that the former tends to occur earlier during the night and begins with a scream. In addition, the child is unable to recall the dream and falls back asleep immediately.

SLEEPWALKING DISORDER

This disorder is characterized by motor movements while asleep. These behaviors may range from sitting up in bed to getting out of bed and performing complex activities such as dressing, opening doors, eating, or going to the bathroom. When sleepwalking, these children have a blank look and are generally unresponsive to attempts at communicating with them, awakening only through major efforts by adults. Parents may report that although their child spoke to them during the episode, speech was poor and no real dialogue occurred. Once awakened, the child with Sleepwalking Disorder appears confused, is disoriented for a few minutes, and is most likely unable to recall the episode of sleepwalking.

Episodes of sleepwalking are more likely to happen during the first part of the night. Because of poor balance and motor coordination during the incident, physical injury to the child or those in close proximity may occur. Social impairment may result because of reluctance to go on overnight visits, such as camp or to the home of friends. Parents are more likely to refer the child when the sleepwalking is frequent, is especially active, involves the risk of physical injury, and leads to the avoidance of overnight social activities.

Sleepwalking may have some of the features associated with Sleep Terror Disorder. When a child gets out of bed during sleep, he or she may actually be trying to flee from a frightening nightmare. When awakened, however, there is no recall of the incident in either disorder. Both disorders may be present at the same time.

This disorder may manifest itself at any age after the child has learned to walk. It is more common for the onset to occur between the ages of 4 and 8 years, with the highest frequency occurring at 12 years of age. Children are more prone to this disorder if there is a familial history of sleepwalking or sleep terrors.

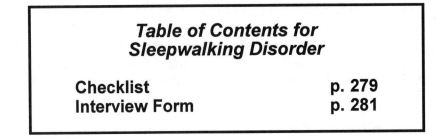

☑ CHECKLIST

SLEEPWALKING DISORDER

```
        +  Presence
KEY     -  Absence
        *  Associated
           Feature
```

MAJOR SYMPTOMS:

-	Inattention
-	Impulsivity
-	Abnormal Activity Level
-	Aggressiveness
-	Violation of Rules
*	Isolation/Withdrawal/Avoidance
-	Inability to Form/Maintain Relationships
-	Disturbances of Affect/Mood
-	Anxiety
-	Depression
-	Delusions/Hallucinations
-	Somatic Complaints
+	Oddities of Behavior
-	Language Impairment
-	Impaired Cognition
+	Significant Distress/Impairment in Important Areas of Functioning

INTERVIEW FORM

SLEEPWALKING DISORDER

1.   For how long has the child been asleep before the onset of the episode?

2.   Describe the child's responses to attempts at arousal.

3.   Does the child remember the episode?   ☐ Yes ☐ No

4.   When the child wakes up, is he or she confused or disoriented?   ☐ Yes ☐ No   If yes, for how long?

5.   Do sleepwalking-like behaviors occur during waking hours?   ☐ Yes ☐ No

6.   Is there a familial history of sleep disturbances?
      ☐ Yes ☐ No

7.   Has the child recently been under stress or overly fatigued?
      ☐ Yes ☐ No

8.   Is the child taking medication?   ☐ Yes ☐ No
      If yes, what kind and when is it taken?

9.   Is the child reluctant to go on overnight visits?
      ☐ Yes ☐ No

10.   Does the child suffer from seizures or Central Nervous System complications?   ☐ Yes ☐ No

TIC
DISORDERS

TIC DISORDERS

There are very few changes from the *DSM-III-R* to the *DSM-IV* for Tourette's Disorder and Chronic Motor or Vocal Tic Disorder. These changes involve the duration of the symptoms before classification of the disorder can be made. Transient Tic Disorder, on the other hand, has undergone significant changes in criteria for diagnosis, from including only simple, single tics in the *DSM-III-R,* to single or multiple motor and/or vocal tics in the *DSM-IV.*

All Tic Disorders are characterized by abnormalities in gross motor movement. Tics are defined as involuntary, rapid production of noises, words, or muscle movements. They may be controlled for a certain period of time despite their compelling nature.

Both motor and vocal tics may be classified as simple or complex. Simple motor tics include eye blinking, neck jerking, shoulder shrugging, and facial grimacing. Simple vocal tics may include coughing, throat clearing, grunting, sniffing, snorting, and barking. Complex motor tics include facial gestures, grooming behaviors, hitting or biting oneself, jumping, touching, stomping, smelling an object, or mimicking someone else. Complex vocal tics involve repetition of words or phrases out of context, use of socially unacceptable words, echolalia, and repeating oneself.

Self-consciousness, embarrassment, and social alienation are common. Impairment in such daily activities as reading and writing may occur as a result of tics. In general, tics tend to decrease during nonanxious, concentrated activities and during sleep, while generally increasing during periods of stress and tension.

TOURETTE'S DISORDER

This disorder involves a multiple tic condition. It is characterized by muscle tics, particularly of the head, torso, and limbs, and by vocal tics. These occur several times a day, nearly every day or intermittently, and should be present for at least 1 year prior to making a diagnosis. The number and combination of simple and complex tics change over time. Vocal tics range from sounds, to grunts, barks, coughs, and words. In a small number of cases utterances of obscenities are present. All of the symptoms tend to appear during stressful situations and lessen during nonanxious events or absorption in an activity, and are not present during sleep.

Other symptoms associated with Tourette's Disorder may involve imitative physical movements, vocalizations, obsessive-compulsive behaviors or thoughts, ritualistic behaviors, and a tendency to repeat words or phrases. Other disorders such as Attention-Deficit/Hyperactivity Disorder, Learning Disorders, and Obsessive-Compulsive Disorder are frequently associated with Tourette's Disorder. Children with Tourette's Disorder are often described as irritable, with low frustration tolerance and attentional problems. They tend to show slower overall maturational processes yet often have at least an average IQ.

The social and emotional consequences of this disorder may range from discomfort in social situations to more serious depressive and suicidal tendencies. Other complications may include physical injury as a result of behaviors associated with complex motor tics, such as head banging, hitting oneself, sudden head jerking, or picking one's skin until it bleeds.

☑ CHECKLIST
TOURETTE'S DISORDER

```
        +  Presence
KEY     -  Absence
        *  Associated
           Feature
```

MAJOR SYMPTOMS:

*	Inattention
*	Impulsivity
*	Abnormal Activity Level
-	Aggressiveness
-	Violation of Rules
*	Isolation/Withdrawal/Avoidance
*	Inability to Form/Maintain Relationships
-	Disturbances of Affect/Mood
*	Anxiety
*	Depression
-	Delusions/Hallucinations
-	Somatic Complaints
+	Oddities of Behavior
-	Language Impairment
-	Impaired Cognition
+	Significant Distress/Impairment in Important Areas of Functioning

INTERVIEW FORM
TOURETTE'S DISORDER

1. Does the child exhibit physical tics?   ☐ Yes ☐ No
   Describe.

2. Does the child vocalize strange noises, such as grunts, yelps, clicks, or barks?   ☐ Yes ☐ No

3. Does the child vocalize obscenities without provocation?
   ☐ Yes ☐ No

4. How often do the physical and/or vocal tics occur?

5. For how long has the child been exhibiting these involuntary behaviors?

6. Does the child imitate the movements or utterances of others?   ☐ Yes ☐ No

7. Does he or she exhibit obsessive-compulsive behaviors, such as constant self-doubt, need to touch things, or need to perform complex physical movements?
   ☐ Yes ☐ No

8. Is the child able to voluntarily control the physical and vocal tics?   ☐ Yes ☐ No   If yes, for how long?

9. Has a medical examination shown neurological abnormalities?   ☐ Yes ☐ No

10. Do the symptoms occur exclusively during substance intoxication?   ☐ Yes ☐ No

11. Describe the degree of social/academic impairment being experienced by the child.

CASE SUMMARY
TOURETTE'S DISORDER
Bob, C.A. 13–1

Reason for Referral: Bob's social studies teacher referred him for evaluation because she had observed nervous mannerisms, such as facial tics and guttural sounds, and felt that his achievement level was significantly below intellectual potential. Bob had previously been evaluated. At that time, his cognitive functioning was found to be in the average range although he showed signs of excessive emotionality.

Behavioral Observations: Bob was observed in the social studies class; he tossed his head, squinted, and uttered monosyllabic sounds in what appeared to be an involuntary rhythmic pattern. In the evaluative situation, Bob was attentive and cooperative. A combination of tic-like phenomena began midway through the first subtest, consisting of eye blinking, grimacing, and short "hup, hup" sounds that he attempted to cover up by saying "Oh gosh." This continued through the remainder of testing. At the second session, he was again able to control the distracting behaviors for about 15 minutes, but this time his short "barked" words seemed to be coprolelic in nature.

Test Interpretations: On the WISC-III Bob earned Verbal, Performance, and Full Scale scores in the Average range of cognitive ability. Bob's reproductions of the Bender Gestalt were without error. He worked carefully and slowly, making several auto-critical comments. There was an obsessive-compulsive flavor to his drawings.

Additional projective testing suggested that Bob's feelings of inadequacy and isolation generate a sense of anger, depression, and frustration. His main defenses appear to be regression and fantasy.

Recommendations: It is strongly recommended that Bob's parents schedule him for a thorough neurological examination to confirm or rule out what may be a physical disorder for which there could be appropriate medication. There are indications that Bob may be a youngster of bright average potential, but the cluster of symptoms he manifests may be interfering with his expected social and academic development.

Neurologist's Diagnosis: I have been following Bob for a period of 8 months and have him on Haldol because of a Tic Disorder. All indications are that he has Tourette's Disorder.

AUTHORS' COMMENTS: Bob presents the typical symptoms of Tourette's Disorder: facial tics, guttural sounds, vocalization of obscenities, as well as attempts at controlling such behaviors. Associated features described in Bob's protocol include obsessive-compulsive behaviors, low self-esteem, anxiety, and depression. Bob's multiple tics were more evident during times of particular stress, especially during formal testing.

Impairment in academic performance has been noted. The extent of his social impairment is not clear from the report. There is no indication as to the duration, frequency, and intensity of the tic behaviors.

CHRONIC MOTOR OR VOCAL TIC DISORDER

The severity and consequent functional impairment of this disorder is less significant than in Tourette's Disorder because the latter involves both multiple motor and vocal tics; the former is characterized by either single or multiple motor or vocal tics, but not both. These may occur several times a day, nearly every day or intermittently, and should be present for at least 1 year, with no more than a 3-month symptom-free period in order to meet diagnostic criteria. Although the symptoms and accompanying impairment are less severe in Chronic Motor or Vocal Tic Disorder, the degree of distress is significant to the individual.

☑ CHECKLIST

CHRONIC MOTOR OR VOCAL TIC DISORDER

KEY	+ Presence
	- Absence
	* Associated Feature

MAJOR SYMPTOMS:

- **-** Inattention
- ***** Impulsivity
- ***** Abnormal Activity Level
- **-** Aggressiveness
- **-** Violation of Rules
- ***** Isolation/Withdrawal/Avoidance
- **-** Inability to Form/Maintain Relationships
- **-** Disturbances of Affect/Mood
- ***** Anxiety
- **-** Depression
- **-** Delusions/Hallucinations
- **-** Somatic Complaints
- **+** Oddities of Behavior
- **-** Language Impairment
- **-** Impaired Cognition
- **+** Significant Distress/Impairment in Important Areas of Functioning

INTERVIEW FORM
CHRONIC MOTOR OR VOCAL TIC DISORDER

1. Describe the type of tics observed in the person.

2. How often do these tics occur?

3. How long have these tics been evident?

4. Do the tics occur exclusively during substance abuse?
    ☐ Yes ☐ No

5. Has there been a diagnosis of Central Nervous System disease, such as encephalitis?   ☐ Yes ☐ No

6. Is the person avoiding others as a result of embarrassment?   ☐ Yes ☐ No

7. Do the tics interfere with the person's ability to function in school and/or on a job?   ☐ Yes ☐ No

CASE SUMMARY

CHRONIC MOTOR OR VOCAL TIC DISORDER
Mike, C.A. 9–0

Reason for Referral: Mike is 9-year-old boy who was diagnosed at age 6 with Attention-Deficit Disorder. Ritalin was prescribed, as well as individual and family therapy. After 2 years on Ritalin, Mike began making sniffing sounds and whistling in the classroom. The teacher called these behaviors to Mike's mother's attention, and her concerns were reported to the prescribing physician. Ritalin was stopped; Mike's academic performance and impulse control promptly deteriorated.

Mike was hospitalized to treat both the tics and the Attention-Deficit Disorder and was started on a prescription of Clonidine. His activity level has been significantly reduced, with no evidence of tics. Mike has been able to return to his classroom.

AUTHORS' COMMENTS: This case illustrates the possible side effects of some medications. In Mike's case, Ritalin, a common drug prescribed for Attention-Deficit Disorder, may have contributed to the onset of vocal tics. These subsided once the medication was changed.

TRANSIENT
TIC DISORDER

This disorder involves the presence of simple or multiple motor tics and/or vocal tics, occurring several times a day, almost every day, for at least 4 weeks, but no longer than 1 year. Classification of this disorder is only made if the individual has never met criteria for either Tourette's Disorder or Chronic Motor or Vocal Tic Disorder. Although the symptoms and accompanying impairment are less severe in Transient Tic Disorder, they still cause significant distress to the individual.

☑ CHECKLIST

TRANSIENT TIC DISORDER

	+	Presence
KEY	-	Absence
	*	Associated Feature

MAJOR SYMPTOMS:

-	Inattention
*	Impulsivity
*	Abnormal Activity Level
-	Aggressiveness
-	Violation of Rules
*	Isolation/Withdrawal/Avoidance
-	Inability to Form/Maintain Relationships
-	Disturbances of Affect/Mood
*	Anxiety
-	Depression
-	Delusions/Hallucinations
-	Somatic Complaints
+	Oddities of Behavior
-	Language Impairment
-	Impaired Cognition
+	Significant Distress/Impairment in Important Areas of Functioning

INTERVIEW FORM
TRANSIENT
TIC DISORDER

1. Does the child exhibit recurrent motor or vocal tics?
   ☐ Yes ☐ No

2. How often and for how long do the tics occur?

3. Has the person been diagnosed as having Tourette's Disorder or Chronic Motor or Vocal Tic Disorder?
   ☐ Yes ☐ No

4. Do the tics occur exclusively during substance abuse?
   ☐ Yes ☐ No

5. Is the person avoiding others as a result of embarrassment?   ☐ Yes ☐ No

6. Do the tics interfere with the person's ability to function in school and/or on the job?   ☐ Yes ☐ No

7. Do the tics regularly appear in anticipation of or during periods of stress in the person's life?   ☐ Yes ☐ No

OTHER DISORDERS
OF CHILDHOOD
AND ADOLESCENCE

REACTIVE ATTACHMENT DISORDER OF INFANCY OR EARLY CHILDHOOD

The *DSM-IV* has introduced two subtypes of this disorder: *Inhibited Type* and *Disinhibited Type* depending on the disturbance in social relatedness. Children with this disorder may manifest persistent lack of initiative or response in social situations, such as absence of visual contact or social initiative, and lack of cooperative play and spontaneity (Inhibited Type). Some children may also be excessively familiar with strangers, showing indiscriminate affection (Disinhibited Type). The diagnosis of Reactive Attachment Disorder of Infancy or Early Childhood is made before the age of 5 years.

In infants, this disorder is manifested mostly by lack of attention, interest, or visual or vocal interaction with the caretaker. There is indifference to being held or picked up and no facial expression indicating joy, surprise, fear, or anger. These children may have poor muscle tone, have a weak cry, sleep excessively, have feeding disturbances, and show a general lack of interest in the environment. They are initially brought to the attention of the physician because of their physical failure to grow or because of another physical complication.

To obtain a diagnosis of Reactive Attachment Disorder of Infancy or Early Childhood, a thorough investigation of the quality of care, both physical and emotional, must be undertaken. Such children may have been abused or neglected, may have had several different caretakers, may have been exposed to physical danger, and likely did not receive attention to their basic emotional needs.

Their caregivers may be experiencing significant depression, may lack support from important others, may have disturbances of impulse control, and/or may have been victims of abuse or neglect in childhood. Other factors may include long periods of separation after birth, either because of the infant's placement in an incubator or inability to secure a home for an adoptable child. Further confirmation of the diagnosis of Reactive Attachment Disorder of Infancy or Early Childhood is made by the recovery observed in such children once they are given adequate care and attention.

Table of Contents for
Reactive Attachment Disorder
of Infancy or Early Childhood

☑ CHECKLIST

REACTIVE ATTACHMENT DISORDER OF INFANCY OR EARLY CHILDHOOD

KEY	
+	Presence
-	Absence
*	Associated Feature

MAJOR SYMPTOMS:

*	Inattention
-	Impulsivity
*	Abnormal Activity Level
-	Aggressiveness
-	Violation of Rules
+	Isolation/Withdrawal/Avoidance
+	Inability to Form/Maintain Relationships
*	Disturbances of Affect/Mood
-	Anxiety
-	Depression
-	Delusions/Hallucinations
-	Somatic Complaints
-	Oddities of Behavior
*	Language Impairment
-	Impaired Cognition
*	Significant Distress/Impairment in Important Areas of Functioning

INTERVIEW FORM

REACTIVE ATTACHMENT DISORDER OF INFANCY OR EARLY CHILDHOOD

1. Describe the child's physical condition.

2. Has a physical examination of the child been conducted recently? ☐ Yes ☐ No

3. Describe the child's social relatedness to others.

4. How long has the caretaker known the child?

5. Describe the quality of the relationship between the child and the caretaker.

6. Does the child convey emotions through facial expressions?
   ☐ Yes ☐ No

7. Does the child initiate and/or respond to play activities?
   ☐ Yes ☐ No

8. Does the child show normal alertness, curiosity, and interest in his or her environment? ☐ Yes ☐ No

9. Does the child show disturbances in eating or sleeping patterns? ☐ Yes ☐ No

10. Is there evidence of physical abuse and/or emotional or physical neglect? ☐ Yes ☐ No

CASE SUMMARY

REACTIVE ATTACHMENT DISORDER OF INFANCY OR EARLY CHILDHOOD
Latoya, C.A. 3–2

Reason for Referral: Latoya was brought to the attention of the examiner by the Department of Children and Families after a neighbor reported concerns about her mother's child-rearing practices. The child was observed to be outside during very cold weather dressed in only her bedclothes. When approached, Latoya asked for food and appeared to be very unkempt. The mother is a 19-year-old unemployed woman who receives state assistance. She has a history of emotional difficulties and was placed in multiple foster homes as a child and an adolescent. A recent physical examination of Latoya revealed her weight to be below the 25th percentile for her age.

Impressions: The examiner saw Latoya and her mother together. The mother's interaction with the child was very negative and hostile. She frequently reprimanded Latoya or shouted directions at her expecting her to behave or perform tasks at a level much higher than her developmental age. There was very little eye contact or positive comments directed towards Latoya, and, in fact, her mother reported very little enjoyment being with her daughter.

Latoya's reaction to her mother was to avoid her as much as possible, even though, when engaged in a task or activity, her attention was good. She would walk away from her mother, refuse to play with her, and ignore her directions.

Although Latoya could maintain attention to activities and objects in front of her, when the examiner attempted to interact with her, Latoya could not engage in reciprocal verbal communication. She would not wait her turn or listen to the examiner's questions, would avoid eye contact, and could not seem to tolerate the examiner's presence. There were no instances of spontaneous smiling during the entire examination period, and, when leaving, Latoya did not respond to attempts to say good-bye.

Diagnosis: Reactive Attachment Disorder of Infancy or Early Childhood

AUTHORS' COMMENTS: Latoya's behavior illustrates many of the characteristics of this disorder. She is unresponsive or avoidant of adults around her and seems to be unable to convey emotions either through verbal or facial expressions. Although she can focus and is alert to tasks, she cannot tolerate closeness from others. Observations of Latoya and her mother are suggestive of interaction that seems to be non-reciprocal and rigid, with little joy expressed by either one. Furthermore, there is evidence of physical neglect and a parental background that might predispose the mother to exhibit poor parenting skills.

GENDER IDENTITY DISORDER

The *DSM-IV* states with great clarity that this disorder must cause a high degree of emotional discomfort or impairment in functioning in order to meet diagnostic criteria. When the disturbance is recognized during childhood, it is identified as Gender Identity Disorder in Children. At later ages, this disorder is identified as Gender Identity Disorder in Adolescents or Adults.

Gender Identity Disorder for both sexes is manifested by feelings of extreme uneasiness, rejection of their own physical sex attributes, and strong proclivity to be of the other sex. This disorder is differentiated from the usual tomboyish or sissy-like behaviors observed in many children by the significant degree of rejection of their own sex assignment as well as identification with the opposite sex.

For boys there is intense interest in feminine clothing and such traditional feminine roles and activities as playing house, playing with dolls, dressing up in women's clothing, and the desire to be included in groups of girls. They may prefer popular female characters on television and in movies, may spend time drawing pretty females, or may choose the role of mother when playing. Boys with this disorder avoid same-sex groups, interests (such as cops and robbers, cars and trucks, and fire engines), and such activities as sports and rough outdoor playing. Aside from typically feminine pursuits and interests, there is a strong and pervasive denial of their physical sex characteristics and a wish that these would disappear. When asked about the future, these boys may state that they expect to be women when they grow up.

For girls, there is strong interest in masculine activities, groups, sports, and rough-and-tumble play. Their fantasy figures are almost always strong, powerful males. There is avoidance of participation in same-sex groups and culturally expected feminine activities. For example, girls may choose not to go to a social activity if it involves wearing a dress. There is also a strong and pervasive denial of their physical sex characteristics and a wish that these would disappear. For example, girls may state that they are biologically unable to bear children. When asked about the future, these girls may state that they expect to be men when they grow up.

This disorder can manifest itself as early as 2 years of age, but referrals are most likely to occur once the child begins school and exhibits some of the behaviors described previously. It is also at this time that isolation and rejection from others begins. This may result in a refusal to attend school, or in later years, to drop out of school. Social impairment for both sexes is significant at home and in school. These children tend to be ostracized and teased by others, especially by those of their same-sex peer group. In addition, the failure to meet parental expectations for gender role identification may result in significant conflicts at home, further isolating the youngster. The lack of acceptance and support by family and peers, and their own psychological distress may lead to depression and suicide attempts.

Table of Contents for
Gender Identity Disorder

☑ CHECKLIST

GENDER IDENTITY DISORDER

KEY	+	Presence
	-	Absence
	*	Associated Feature

MAJOR SYMPTOMS:

-	**Inattention**
-	**Impulsivity**
-	**Abnormal Activity Level**
-	**Aggressiveness**
-	**Violation of Rules**
*	**Isolation/Withdrawal/Avoidance**
*	**Inability to Form/Maintain Relationships**
-	**Disturbances of Affect/Mood**
*	**Anxiety**
*	**Depression**
-	**Delusions/Hallucinations**
-	**Somatic Complaints**
+	**Oddities of Behavior**
-	**Language Impairment**
-	**Impaired Cognition**
+	**Significant Distress/Impairment in Important Areas of Functioning**

INTERVIEW FORM
GENDER IDENTITY DISORDER
For Males

1. Does the boy state a strong desire to be a girl or insist that he is a girl?   ☐ Yes ☐ No

2. Does the boy persistently negate male anatomical features as evidenced by any of the following?

    ♦ That he will grow up to become a woman
       ☐ Yes ☐ No

    ♦ That his penis or testes are repugnant or will disappear   ☐ Yes ☐ No

    ♦ That it would be better not to have a penis or testes
       ☐ Yes ☐ No

3. Is the boy overly preoccupied with such female activities as participation in girls' games?   ☐ Yes ☐ No

4. Does he engage in cross-dressing?   ☐ Yes ☐ No

5. Does he avoid participating in activities with same-sex groups?   ☐ Yes ☐ No

6. Describe his play activities, interests, and choice of toys.

7. Has the boy reached puberty?   ☐ Yes ☐ No

8. Describe how family members and friends react to the boy's tendencies towards feminine interests and behaviors.

9. Has there been refusal to attend school?   ☐ Yes ☐ No

10. Is there evidence of significant emotional discomfort and/or impairment in social, school, or occupational functioning? ☐ Yes ☐ No

INTERVIEW FORM
GENDER IDENTITY DISORDER
For Females

1. Does the girl state a strong desire to be a boy or insist that she is a boy?   ☐ Yes ☐ No

2. Does the girl persistently negate feminine anatomical features as evidenced by any of the following?

    ♦ Asserts that she has or will grow a penis
      ☐ Yes ☐ No

    ♦ Refuses to urinate in a sitting position
      ☐ Yes ☐ No

    ♦ Asserts that she does not want to grow breasts or menstruate   ☐ Yes ☐ No

3. Does the girl persistently refuse to wear feminine clothing and insist upon wearing typically masculine clothing instead?   ☐ Yes ☐ No

4. Does she avoid participating in activities with same-sex groups?   ☐ Yes ☐ No

5. Has the girl reached puberty?   ☐ Yes ☐ No

6. Describe how family members and friends react to the girl's tendencies towards masculine interests and behaviors.

7. Has there been refusal to attend school?   ☐ Yes ☐ No

8. Is there evidence of significant emotional discomfort and/or impairment in social, school, or occupational functioning?   ☐ Yes ☐ No

CASE SUMMARY

GENDER IDENTITY DISORDER
Mark, C.A. 11–0

Reason for Referral: Mark was referred for evaluation because of excessive absenteeism from school. His parents were divorced when he was 6 months old, and he currently lives with his mother. He is kept at home whenever he has a headache, which occurs several days per week. On the rare days that he does go to school, he is apt to go to the school nurse complaining of a headache. Mark usually remains at home by himself or accompanies his mother to her job. He does not participate in peer group activities but enjoys fishing alone. His only close friend of the same age is a female cousin who lives next door.

During the evaluation, the examiner noted several behaviors which made her feel uncomfortable. Mark would brush his hair away from his face and angle his cheek towards the examiner prior to making a verbal response. He had elaborate hand gestures which had a feminine quality. Mark also showed unusual interest in the examiner's clothes and asked where she had purchased them.

During the clinical interview, Mark stated that he wished to be a girl, explaining that he felt more comfortable participating in activities such as dressing up in his mother's clothing when she wasn't at home. He also disclosed that he has a collection of dolls which he keeps hidden in his closet and with which he only plays when alone or with his cousin. Mark's human figure drawing was a detailed rendering of a female. He refused to draw a male when requested to do so. Mark stated that he was constantly teased by peers in school because he did not want to participate in any sports or group activities with the other boys and because he preferred to stay with the girls during recess and at lunch.

Diagnosis: Upon psychiatric examination, the diagnosis of Gender Identity Disorder was made.

AUTHORS' COMMENTS: Mark's behavior associated with this disorder has caused significant isolation from his peer group and school avoidance. Although it is not clear from the clinical interview the extent of Mark's discomfort with his own male anatomical features, his refusal to draw a male figure does suggest uneasiness associated with his gender identity. This is also supported by his significant interest in female activities, such as his cross-dressing and playing with dolls.

SUMMARY CHECKLIST
OF MAJOR SYMPTOMS

DISORDERS

KEY
+ Presence
- Absence
* Associated Feature

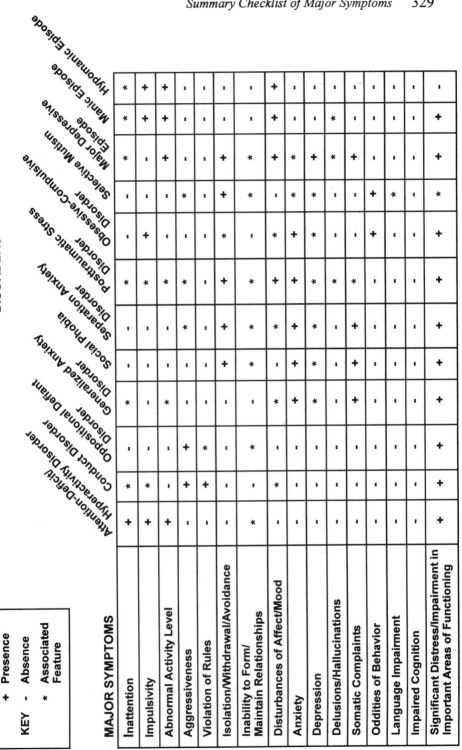

MAJOR SYMPTOMS	Attention-Deficit/Hyperactivity Disorder	Conduct Disorder	Oppositional Defiant Disorder	Generalized Anxiety Disorder	Social Phobia	Separation Anxiety Disorder	Posttraumatic Stress Disorder	Obsessive-Compulsive Disorder	Selective Mutism	Major Depressive Episode	Manic Episode	Hypomanic Episode
Inattention	+	*	*	-	-	-	*	-	-	*	*	*
Impulsivity	+	*	-	-	-	-	*	+	-	-	+	+
Abnormal Activity Level	+	-	*	-	-	-	*	-	-	+	+	+
Aggressiveness	-	+	-	-	-	*	*	-	*	-	-	-
Violation of Rules	-	+	-	-	-	-	-	-	-	-	-	-
Isolation/Withdrawal/Avoidance	-	-	-	+	+	+	+	*	+	+	-	-
Inability to Form/Maintain Relationships	*	-	-	*	*	*	*	-	*	*	-	-
Disturbances of Affect/Mood	-	-	*	-	-	*	+	*	-	+	+	+
Anxiety	-	-	+	+	+	+	+	+	*	*	-	-
Depression	-	-	*	*	*	*	*	*	*	+	-	-
Delusions/Hallucinations	-	-	-	-	-	-	*	-	-	*	*	-
Somatic Complaints	-	-	+	+	+	+	-	-	-	+	-	-
Oddities of Behavior	-	-	-	-	-	-	-	+	+	-	-	-
Language Impairment	-	-	-	-	-	-	-	*	*	-	-	-
Impaired Cognition	-	-	-	-	-	-	-	-	-	-	-	-
Significant Distress/Impairment in Important Areas of Functioning	+	+	+	+	+	+	+	+	*	+	+	-

DISORDERS

KEY
+ Presence
- Absence
* Associated Feature

MAJOR SYMPTOMS	Dysthymic Disorder	Cyclothymic Disorder	Adj. Dis. with Depressed Mood	Adj. Dis. with Anxiety	Adj. Dis. with Mixed Anxiety & Depressed Mood	Adj. Dis. with Disturbance of Conduct	Adj. Dis. with Mixed Disturbance of Emotions & Conduct	Autistic Disorder	Rett's Disorder	Childhood Disintegrative Disorder	Asperger's Disorder	Pica	Rumination Disorder
Inattention	*	*	*	*	*	*	*	-	-	*	*	-	-
Impulsivity	-	+	-	-	*	*	*	-	*	*	*	-	-
Abnormal Activity Level	*	+	*	*	-	*	*	-	*	*	*	-	-
Aggressiveness	-	-	-	-	*	-	-	-	-	-	-	-	-
Violation of Rules	-	-	-	-	+	+	-	-	-	-	-	-	-
Isolation/Withdrawal/Avoidance	*	*	*	-	-	-	+	*	*	*	+	-	-
Inability to Form/ Maintain Relationships	*	-	*	*	*	*	+	+	+	+	+	-	-
Disturbances of Affect/Mood	+	+	+	+	+	-	+	+	+	+	+	-	-
Anxiety	-	-	+	+	*	-	-	-	-	-	-	-	-
Depression	+	+	+	+	*	-	*	-	-	-	-	-	-
Delusions/Hallucinations	-	-	-	-	-	-	-	-	-	-	-	-	-
Somatic Complaints	*	*	-	-	-	-	-	-	-	-	-	-	-
Oddities of Behavior	-	-	-	-	-	-	+	+	+	+	+	+	+
Language Impairment	-	-	-	-	-	-	+	+	+	+	*	-	-
Impaired Cognition	-	-	-	-	-	-	+	+	*	+	*	*	*
Significant Distress/Impairment in Important Areas of Functioning	+	+	+	+	+	+	+	+	+	+	+	-	-

DISORDERS

KEY
+ Presence
- Absence
* Associated Feature

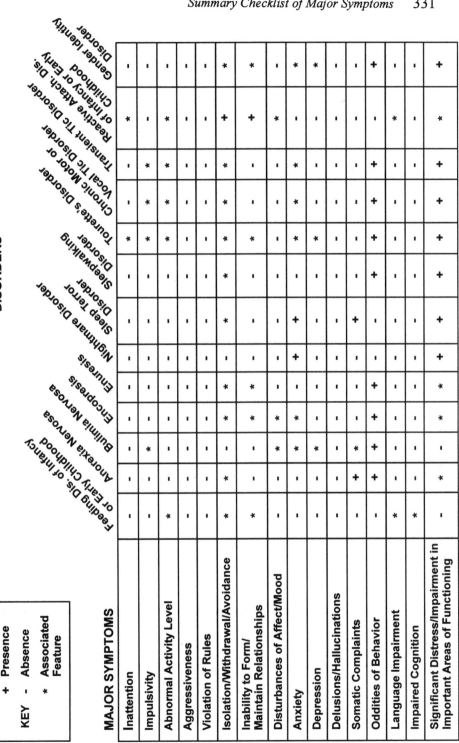

MAJOR SYMPTOMS	Feeding Dis. of Infancy or Early Childhood	Anorexia Nervosa	Bulimia Nervosa	Encopresis	Enuresis	Nightmare Disorder	Sleep Terror Disorder	Sleepwalking Disorder	Tourette's Disorder	Chronic Motor or Vocal Tic Disorder	Transient Tic Disorder	Reactive Attach. Dis. of Infancy or Early Childhood	Gender Identity Disorder
Inattention	-	-	-	-	-	-	-	-	*	-	-	*	-
Impulsivity	-	*	*	-	-	-	-	*	*	*	*	-	-
Abnormal Activity Level	*	-	-	-	-	-	-	*	*	*	*	*	-
Aggressiveness	-	-	-	-	-	-	-	-	-	-	-	-	-
Violation of Rules	-	-	-	-	-	-	-	-	-	-	-	-	-
Isolation/Withdrawal/Avoidance	*	*	*	*	-	*	*	*	*	*	*	+	*
Inability to Form/Maintain Relationships	*	-	-	*	-	-	-	-	*	-	-	+	*
Disturbances of Affect/Mood	-	*	*	-	-	-	-	-	-	-	*	*	-
Anxiety	-	*	*	*	+	+	+	-	*	*	-	-	*
Depression	-	*	*	-	-	-	-	-	*	-	-	-	*
Delusions/Hallucinations	-	-	-	-	-	-	-	-	-	-	-	-	-
Somatic Complaints	-	*	-	-	-	-	+	-	-	-	-	-	-
Oddities of Behavior	-	+	+	+	-	-	-	+	+	+	+	-	+
Language Impairment	*	-	-	-	-	-	-	-	-	-	-	*	-
Impaired Cognition	*	-	-	-	-	-	-	-	-	-	-	-	-
Significant Distress/Impairment in Important Areas of Functioning	-	*	*	*	+	+	+	+	+	+	+	*	+

GLOSSARY OF
MAJOR SYMPTOMS

GLOSSARY OF MAJOR SYMPTOMS

Abnormal Activity Level: Hyperactivity or hypoactivity going beyond an expected norm.

Affect: An observable manifestation of an emotion. Affect may be recognized by the tone of voice, physical expression, body language, and altered behavioral responses.

Aggressiveness: Unprovoked verbal and/or physical attacks on people and/or property.

Anxiety: Generally defined as an advanced response to threat not necessarily objectively apparent. It distinguishes itself from fear in that the latter is more likely to concern itself with known and external sources of danger. Despite their differing sources, fear and anxiety manifest themselves in a similar manner, involving autonomic hyperactivity, tension, apprehension, and a state of tense alertness.

Delusion: A firmly and consistently held affirmation of a belief which is not supported by reality or by generally accepted perceptions, or which is held in spite of objective evidence. The delusional belief is divergent from the cultural norms of the individual holding it.

Depression: Marked by sadness, inactivity, feelings of dejection, and self-deprecation.

Hallucinations: A perception attributed to the senses, which is in fact not derived from them. It may be differentiated from illusions by the fact that the latter are misinterpretations or distortions of external stimuli.

Impaired Cognition: It may include loosening of associations, incoherence, poverty of content of speech, neologisms, perseveration, blocking, or below-average IQ.

Impulsivity: A spontaneous inclination to perform an unpremeditated action. The action usually has a sudden, forceful, compelling quality and is taken without consideration for the consequences.

Inability to Form/Maintain Relationships: Incapacity to establish or continue relationships, or social avoidance of the individual by others as a result of his or her behaviors.

Inattention: The inability to maintain concentration on an object, task, or activity. The extent of deviation from such would be a measure of distractibility and inadequate attention.

Isolation/Withdrawal/Avoidance: Failure to approach others or situations because of fear, inexperience, lack of confidence, absorption in solitary activities, or social discomfort. Also may include intentional refusal to speak.

Language Impairment: Failure to reach expected language milestones, speech impediment, echolalia, or unintelligibility.

Mood: A sustained emotion capable of affecting an individual's perceptions and responses. Common manifestations of mood include euphoria, irritability, anxiety, depression, annoyance, and anger.

Oddities of Behavior: Includes behaviors of such unusual quality that they bring attention to the individual. May include hair pulling, rocking, or other rhythmic movements; motor tics; food hoarding; sleepwalking; or eating nonfood substances. May also involve cross-dressing.

Significant Distress/Impairment in Important Areas of Functioning: Impact of given symptoms on an individual, causing psychological pain and/or inability to meet with requirements and expectations at home, school, job, and/or in social situations.

Somatic Complaints: Complaints of a physical nature, such as nausea, vomiting, headaches, tachycardia, and so on, for which no physical basis can be established.

Violation of Rules: Chronic disregard of a variety of important rules that are reasonable and age-appropriate for the individual at home and/or school, such as truancy, stealing, substance abuse, or precocious sexual activity.

NATIONAL ASSOCIATIONS
AND RESOURCES

NATIONAL ASSOCIATIONS AND RESOURCES

American Academy of Child and Adolescent Psychiatry
3615 Wisconsin Avenue NW
Washington, DC 20016

American Anorexia/Bulimia Association
293 Central Park West, Suite 1R
New York, NY 10024

American Council for Drug Education
c/o Phoenix House
164 W. 74th Street
New York, NY 10023

American Council on Alcoholism (ACA)
2522 St. Paul Street
Baltimore, MD 21218

American Speech-Language-Hearing Association
10801 Rockville Pke
Rockville, MD 20852

Anxiety Disorders Association of America
11900 Parklawn Drive, Suite 100
Rockville, MD 20852-2624

Autism Network International
PO Box 448
Syracuse, NY 13210-0448

Autism Services Center
Prichard Building
605 9th Street
PO Box 507
Huntington, WV 25710-0507

Autism Society of America
7910 Woodmont Avenue, Suite 650
Bethesda, MD 20814-3015

Children and Adults with Attention Deficit Disorders (CHADD)
499 NW 70th Avenue, Suite 101
Plantation, FL 33317

Children of Alcoholics Foundation
PO Box 4185
Grand Central Station
New York, NY 10163-4185

Council for Children with Behavioral Disorders
c/o Council for Exceptional Children
1920 Association Drive
Reston, VA 22091

Council on Anxiety Disorders
Route 1, Box 1364
Clarkesville, GA 30523

Depression and Related Affective Disorders Association
John Hopkins Hospital, Meyer 3-181
600 N. Wolfe Street
Baltimore, MD 21205

International Rett Syndrome Association
9121 Piscataway Road, No. 2B
Clinton, MD 20735

International Society for Traumatic Stress Studies
60 Revere Drive, Suite 500
Northbrook, IL 60062

**National Association of Anorexia Nervosa and Associated
    Disorders**
Box 7
Highland Park, IL 60035

National Attention-Deficit Disorder Association
PO Box 972
Mentor, OH 44061-0972

National Depressive and Manic Depressive Association
730 N. Franklin, Suite 501
Chicago, IL 60610

National Foundation for Depressive Illness
PO Box 2257
New York, NY 10116

National Mental Health Association (NMHA)
1021 Prince Street
Alexandria, VA 22314-2971

Obsessive Compulsive Foundation
PO Box 70
Milford, CT 06460-0070

Selective Mutism Foundation
PO Box 450632
Sunrise, FL 33345

Sex Information and Education Council of the U.S.
130 W. 42nd Street, Suite 2500
New York, NY 10036

Stanley Foundation Bipolar Network
5430 Grosvenor Lane, Suite 200
Bethesda, MD 20814

Tourette Syndrome Association
42-40 Bell Boulevard
Bayside, NY 11361

World Federation for Mental Health
1021 Prince Street
Alexandria, VA 22314

**Zero to Three/National Center for Clinical Infant Programs
    (NCCIP)**
734 15th Street NW, No. 10
Washington, DC 20005-1013

ADDITIONAL
READINGS

ADDITIONAL READINGS

DISRUPTIVE BEHAVIOR DISORDERS

Achenbach, T. M. (1982). *Developmental Psychopathology* (2nd ed.). New York: John Wiley.

Barkley, R. A. (1987). *Defiant Children.* New York: Guilford.

Barkley, R. A. (1990). *Attention-Deficit Hyperactivity Disorder: A Handbook for Diagnosis and Treatment.* New York: Guilford.

Breen, M. J., & Altepetter, T. S. (1990). *Disruptive Behavior Disorders in Children.* New York: Guilford.

DuPaul, G. J., & Stoner, G. (1994). *ADHD in the Schools.* New York: Guilford.

Goldstein, A. P., Harootunian, B., & Conoley, J. C. (1994). *Student Aggression: Prevention, Management, and Replacement Training.* New York: Guilford.

Goldstein, S., & Goldstein, M. (1990). *Managing Attention Disorders in Children.* New York: John Wiley.

Henggeler, S. W. (1989). *Delinquency in Adolescence.* Thousand Oaks, CA: Sage.

Kaminer, Y. (1994). *Adolescent Substance Abuse: A Comprehensive Guide to Theory and Practice.* New York: Plenum.

Kazdin, A. E. (1995). *Conduct Disorders in Childhood and Adolescence* (2nd ed.). Thousand Oaks, CA: Sage.

McConaughy, S. H., & Skiba, R. J. (1993). Comorbidity of internalizing and externalizing problems. *School Psychology Review, 22,* 421-436.

Quay, H. C. (1986). Conduct disorders. In H. C. Quay & J. S. Werry (Eds.), *Psychopathological Disorders of Childhood* (3rd ed., pp. 35-72). New York: John Wiley.

ANXIETY DISORDERS

Beck, A. T., Emery, G., with Greenberg, R. (1985). *Anxiety Disorders and Phobias: A Cognitive Perspective.* New York: Basic Books.

Kendall, P. C., Chansky, T. E., Kane, M. T., Kim, R. S., Kortlander, E., Ronan, K. R., Sessa, F. M., & Siqueland, L. (1992). *Anxiety Disorders in Youth: Cognitive Behavioral Interventions.* Boston: Allyn & Bacon.

King, N. J. (1988). *Children's Phobias: A Behavioral Perspective.* New York: John Wiley.

King, N. J., Ollendick, T. H., & Tonge, B. J. (1995). *School Refusal: Assessment and Treatment.* Boston: Allyn & Bacon.

Klein, R. G., & Last, C. G. (1989). *Anxiety Disorders in Children.* Thousand Oaks, CA: Sage.

March, J. S. (Ed.). (1995). *Anxiety Disorders in Children and Adolescents.* New York: Guilford.

Ollendick, T. H., King, N. J., & Yule, W. (1994). *International Handbook of Phobic and Anxiety Disorders in Children and Adolescents.* New York: Plenum.

Ramirez, S. Z., Kratochwill, T. R., & Morris, R. J. (1997). In G. G. Bear, K. M. Minke, & A. Thomas (Eds.), *Children's Needs II: Development, Problems, and Alternatives* (Chapter 28, pp. 315-327). Bethesda, MD: National Association of School Psychologists.

Saigh, P. A. (1992). *Posttraumatic Stress Disorder: A Behavioral Approach to Assessment and Treatment.* Boston: Allyn & Bacon.

Weaver, J. D. (1995). *Disasters: Mental Health Interventions.* Sarasota, FL: Professional Resource Press.

MOOD DISORDERS

Beck, A. T. (1967). *Depression: Clinical, Experimental and Theoretical Aspects.* New York: Hoeber.

Geller, B., & Luby, J. (1997). Child and adolescent bipolar disorder: Review of the past 10 years. *Journal of the American Academy of Child and Adolescent Psychiatry 36*(9), 1-9.

Kazdin, A. E. (1990). Childhood depression. *Journal of Child Psychology & Psychiatry, 31*, 121-160.

Matson, J. L. (1989). *Treating Depression in Children and Adolescents.* New York: Pergamon.

Pfeffer, C. R. (1986). *The Suicidal Child.* New York: Guilford.

Reynolds, W. (Ed.). (1992). *Internalizing Disorders in Children and Adolescents.* New York: John Wiley.

Reynolds, W., & Johnston, H. F. (Eds.). (1994). *A Handbook of Depression in Children and Adolescents.* New York: Plenum.

Rutter, M., & Izard, C. E. (Eds.). (1986). *Depression in Young People: Developmental and Clinical Perspectives.* New York: Guilford.

Shamoo, T. K., & Patros, P. G. (1992). *Helping Your Child Cope with Depression and Suicidal Thoughts.* New York: Lexington.

Stark, K. D. (1990). *Childhood Depression: School-Based Intervention.* New York: Guilford.

Trad, P. V. (1987). *Infant and Childhood Depression: Developmental Factors.* New York: John Wiley.

ADJUSTMENT DISORDERS

Chandler, L. A. (1985). *Children Under Stress: Understanding Emotional Adjustment Reactions* (2nd ed.). Springfield, IL: Richard C. Thomas.

Compas, B. E. (1987). Stress and life events during childhood and adolescence. *Clinical Psychology Review, 7,* 275-302.

Field, T., McCabe, P., & Schneiderman, N. (Eds.). (1985). *Stress and Coping.* Hillsdale, NJ: Lawrence Erlbaum.

Garmezy, N., & Rutter, M. (Eds.). (1983). *Stress, Coping, and Development in Children.* New York: McGraw-Hill.

Monahan, C. (1993). *Children and Trauma: A Parent's Guide to Helping Children Heal.* New York: Lexington Books/The Free Press.

Sorensen, E. S. (1993). *Children's Stress and Coping: A Family Perspective.* New York: Guilford.

PERVASIVE DEVELOPMENTAL DISORDERS

Cohen, D., & Donnellan, A. M. (Eds.). (1987). *Handbook of Autism and Pervasive Developmental Disorders.* New York: John Wiley.

Dawson, G. (Ed.). (1989). *Autism: Nature, Diagnosis, and Treatment.* New York: Guilford.

Groden, G., & Baron, M. G. (Eds.). (1988). *Autism: Strategies for Change: A Comprehensive Approach to the Education and Treatment of Children with Autism and Related Disorders.* New York: Gardner.

Schopler, E., & Mesibov, G. B. (Eds.). (1992). *High-Functioning Individuals with Autism.* New York: Plenum.

Schopler, E., & Mesibov, G. B. (Eds.). (1994). *Behavioral Issues in Autism.* New York: Plenum.

Schopler, E., VanBourgondien, M. E., & Bristol, M. M. (Eds.). (1993). *Preschool Issues in Autism.* New York: Plenum.

Schreibman, L. (1988). *Autism.* Thousand Oaks, CA: Sage.

FEEDING AND EATING DISORDERS

Bicknell, J. D. (1975). *Pica: A Childhood Symptom.* London: Butterworths.

Domangue, B. B., & Field, H. L. (Eds.). (1987). *Eating Disorders Throughout the Life Span.* New York: Praeger.

Fairburn, C. (1995). *Overcoming Binge Eating.* New York: Guilford.

Garner, D. M., & Garfinkel, P. E. (Eds.). (1984). *Handbook of Psychotherapy for Anorexia Nervosa and Bulimia.* New York: Guilford.

Giannini, J. A., & Slaby, A. E. (1993). *The Eating Disorders.* New York: Springer-Verlag.

Hsu, L. K. G. (1990). *Eating Disorders.* New York: Guilford.

Lyman, R. D., & Hembree-Kigin, T. L. (1994). *Mental Health Interventions with Preschool Children.* New York: Plenum.

Marchi, M., & Cohen, P. (1990). Early childhood eating behaviors and adolescent eating disorders. *Journal of the American Academy of Child & Adolescent Psychiatry, 29,* 112-117.

ELIMINATION DISORDERS

Butler, R. J. (1987). *Nocturnal Enuresis: Psychological Perspectives.* Bristol, England: Wright.

Christophersen, E. (1994). *Pediatric Compliance: A Guide for the Primary Care Physician.* New York: Plenum.

Lyman, R. D., & Hembree-Kigin, T. L. (1994). *Mental Health Interventions with Preschool Children.* New York: Plenum.

Mellon, M., & Houts, A. (1995). Elimination disorder. In R. Ammerman & M. Hersen (Eds.), *Handbook of Child Behavior Therapy in the Psychiatric Setting* (pp. 341-365). New York: John Wiley.

Schaefer, C. E. (1979). *Childhood Encopresis and Enuresis: Causes and Therapy.* New York: Van Nostrand Reinhold.

SLEEP DISORDERS

Ablon, S. L., & Mack, J. E. (1979). Sleep disorders. In J. Noshpitz (Ed.), *Basic Handbook of Child Psychiatry* (Vol. 2, pp. 643-660). New York: Basic Books.

Adair, R. H., & Bauchner, H. (1993). Sleep problems in childhood. *Current Problems in Pediatrics,* 147-170.

Guilleminault, C. (Ed.). (1987). *Sleep and Its Disorders in Children.* New York: Raven Press.

Kales, J. D., Kales, A., & Soldatos, C. R. (1980). Night terrors: Clinical characteristics and personality patterns. *Archives of General Psychiatry, 37,* 1413-1421.

Lyman, R. D., & Hembree-Kigin, T. L. (1994). *Mental Health Interventions with Preschool Children.* New York: Plenum.

Mindell, J. A. (1993). Sleep disorders in children. *Health Psychology, 12*(2), 151-162.

TIC DISORDERS

Cohen, D. J., Bruun, R., & Leckman, J. (Eds.). (1988). *Tourette's Syndrome and Tic Disorders: Clinical Understanding and Treatment.* New York: John Wiley.

Comings, D. E. (1990). *Tourette Syndrome and Human Behavior.* Duarte, CA: Hope Press.

Kurlan, R. (Ed.). (1993). *Handbook of Tourette's Syndrome and Related Tic and Behavioral Disorders.* New York: Marcel Dekker.

Lees, A. J. (1985). *Tics and Related Disorders.* New York: Churchill Livingstone.

Singer, H. S., & Walkup, J. T. (1991) Tourette syndrome and other tic disorders: Diagnosis, pathophysiology, and treatment. *Medicine, 70,* 15-32.

REACTIVE ATTACHMENT DISORDER OF INFANCY OR EARLY CHILDHOOD

Ainsworth, M., Blehar, M., Waters, E., & Wall, S. (1978). *Patterns of Attachment.* Hillsdale, NJ: Lawrence Erlbaum.

Bowlby, J. (1980). *Attachment and Loss.* New York: Basic Books.

Diagnostic Classification of Mental Health and Developmental Disorders of Infancy and Early Childhood. (1994). Arlington, VA: Zero to Three/National Center for Clinical Infant Programs.

Fraiberg, S., Adelson, E., & Shapiro, V. (1980). Ghosts in the nursery: A psychoanalytic approach to the problems of impaired infant-mother relationships. In S. Fraiberg (Ed.), *Clinical Studies in Infant Mental Health* (pp. 164-196). New York: Basic Books.

James, B. (1994). *Handbook for Treatment of Attachment-Trauma Problems in Children.* New York: Lexington Books/The Free Press.

Starr, R. H., Jr., & Wolfe, D. A. (1991). *The Effects of Child Abuse and Neglect: Issues and Research.* New York: Guilford.

GENDER IDENTITY DISORDER

Constantine, L. L., & Martinson, F. M. (Eds.). (1981). *Children and Sex: New Findings, New Perspectives.* Boston: Little, Brown.

Gordon, B. N., & Schroeder, C. S. (1995). *Sexuality: A Developmental Approach to Problems.* New York: Plenum.

Rekers, G. A. (1991). Development of problems of puberty and sex roles in adolescence. In C. C. Walker & M. C. Roberts (Eds.), *Handbook of Clinical Child Psychology* (2nd ed., pp. 607-622). New York: John Wiley.

Zucker, K. J., & Bradley, S. J. (1995). *Gender Idenitity Disorder and Psychosexual Problems in Children and Adolescents.* New York: Guilford.

INDEX

INDEX

If You Found This Book Useful . . .

You might want to know more about our other titles.

If you would like to receive our latest catalog, please return this form:

Name:_____
(Please Print)

Address:_____

Address:_____

City/State/Zip:_____
This is ❑ home ❑ office

Telephone:(_____)_____

I am a:

_____ Psychologist	_____ Mental Health Counselor
_____ Psychiatrist	_____ Marriage and Family Therapist
_____ School Psychologist	_____ Not in Mental Health Field
_____ Clinical Social Worker	_____ Other:_____

◆   ◆   ◆

Professional Resource Press
P.O. Box 15560
Sarasota, FL 34277-1560

Telephone #800-443-3364
FAX #941-343-9201
E-mail at mail@prpress.com

Add A Colleague To Our Mailing List . . .

If you would like us to send our latest catalog to one of your colleagues, please return this form.

Name:_____
(Please Print)

Address:_____

Address:_____

City/State/Zip:_____
This is ☐ home ☐ office

Telephone:(_____)_____

This person is a:

_____ Psychologist   _____ Mental Health Counselor
_____ Psychiatrist   _____ Marriage and Family Therapist
_____ School Psychologist   _____ Not in Mental Health Field
_____ Clinical Social Worker   _____ Other:_____

Name of person completing this form:_____

◆   ◆   ◆

Professional Resource Press
P.O. Box 15560
Sarasota, FL 34277-1560

Telephone #800-443-3364
FAX #941-343-9201
E-mail at mail@prpress.com

CES2/9/98